really easy piano

THE Beatles COLLECTION

ISBN: 978-1-70512-134-4

HAL•LEONARD®

Visit Hal Leonard Online at
www.halleonard.com

Contact us:
Hal Leonard
7777 West Bluemound Road
Milwaukee, WI 53213
Email: info@halleonard.com

In Europe, contact:
Hal Leonard Europe Limited
42 Wigmore Street
Marylebone, London, W1U 2RY
Email: info@halleonardeurope.com

In Australia, contact:
Hal Leonard Australia Pty. Ltd.
4 Lentara Court
Cheltenham, Victoria, 3192 Australia
Email: info@halleonard.com.au

THE BEATLES COLLECTION

really easy piano

THE BEATLES COLLECTION

And I Love Her

Words and Music by John Lennon and Paul McCartney

Described by McCartney as "the first song that I impressed myself with", 'And I Love Her' comes from the band's 1964 album, *A Hard Day's Night*. McCartney was with girlfriend Jane Asher at the time but has never said whether the song was written about her. It is also one of the only Beatles tracks that has just one vocalist on the record – usually the lead vocal duties are split between Lennon and McCartney.

Hints & Tips: The intro is almost like a fanfare. Remember the B♭ in the key signature.
The left-hand drives the music forward.

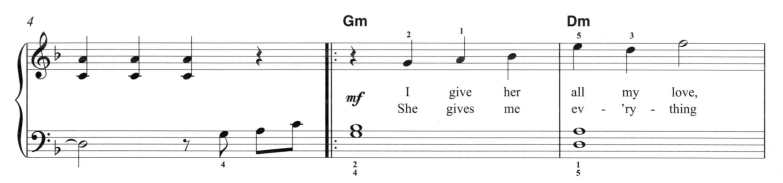

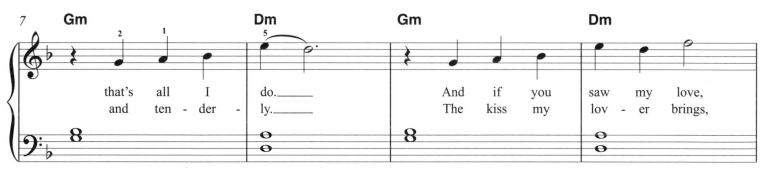

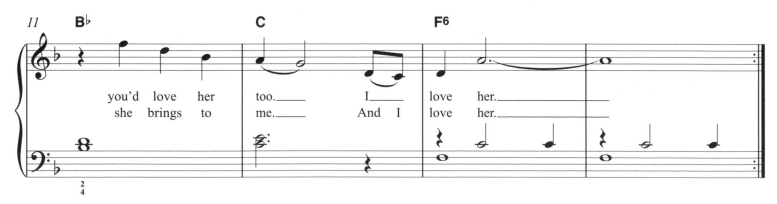

A love like ours could nev - er die as long as

I have you near me. Bright are the stars that shine,

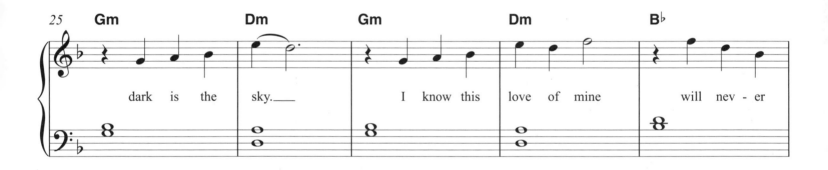

dark is the sky. I know this love of mine will nev - er

die. And I love her.

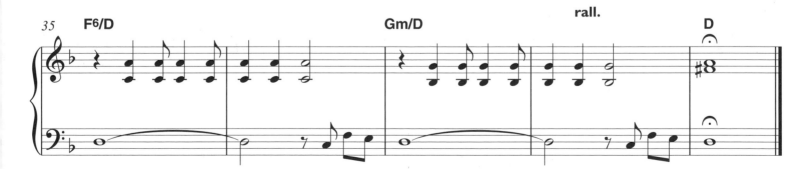

All You Need Is Love

Words and Music by John Lennon and Paul McCartney

'All You Need Is Love' was written in 1967 for the BBC's global production *Our World* which showcased live broadcasts from around the world. The song's strong message at a time of conflict immediately popularized the hit.

Hints & Tips: Notice that the quavers (eighth notes) are to be played in Swing style. First learn the right hand alone, then look out for the descending left-hand pattern: G, F♯, E, starting in bar 4 and continuing throughout.

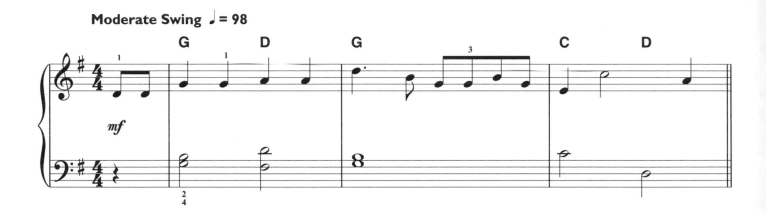

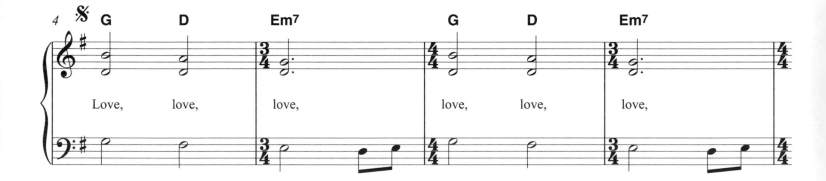

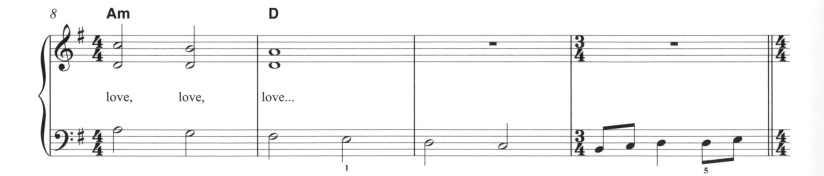

There's noth-ing you can do that can't be done.
Noth-ing you can make that can't be made.
Noth-ing you can know that is-n't known.

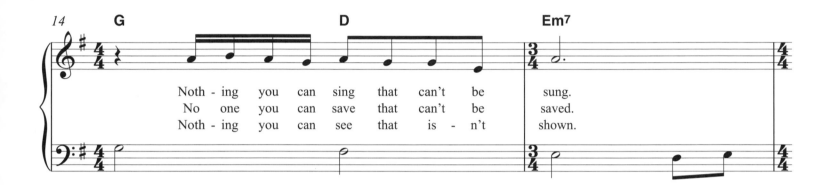

Noth-ing you can sing that can't be sung.
No one you can save that can't be saved.
Noth-ing you can see that is-n't shown.

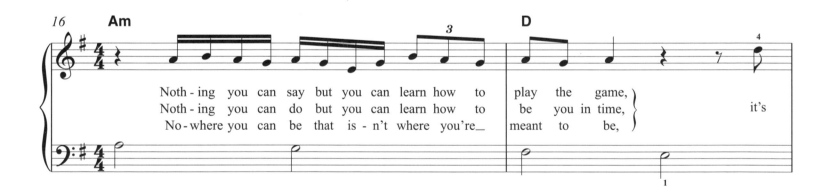

Noth-ing you can say but you can learn how to play the game,
Noth-ing you can do but you can learn how to be you in time,
No-where you can be that is-n't where you're meant to be,

it's

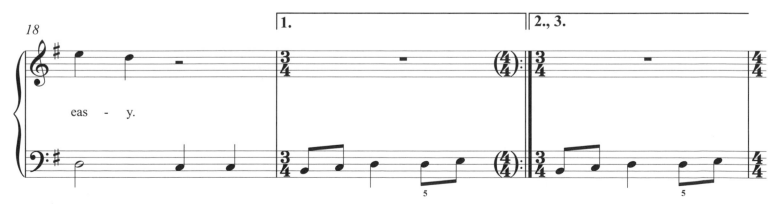

eas - y.

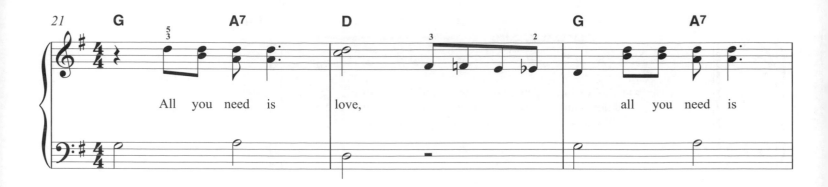

All you need is love, all you need is

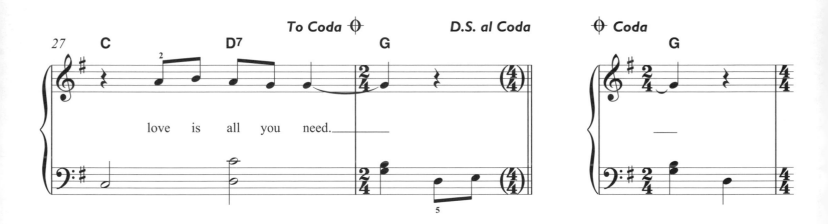

love, all you need is love, love,

To Coda ✛   *D.S. al Coda*   ✛ *Coda*

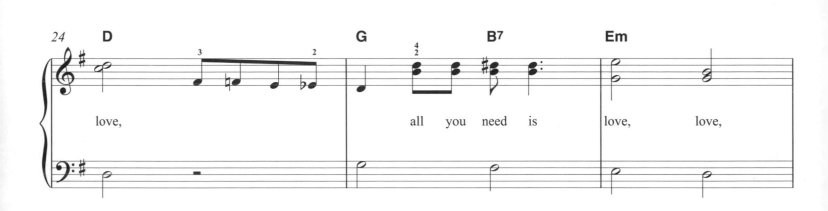

love is all you need.

Love is all you need.   Love is all you need.   Love is all you need.

Come Together

Words and Music by John Lennon and Paul McCartney

This song came about when psychologist Timothy Leary set up his campaign to become
Governor of California in 1969 and asked Lennon to write a song to support his slogan,
'Come together, join the party'. Though Lennon wrote 'Come Together' with the campaign in
mind, the song did not end up being used, instead making it onto the 1969 album, *Abbey Road*.

**Hints & Tips: The left hand should keep a steady, heavy beat in the verse.
The right hand often plays two notes; make sure they sound exactly together.**

Slow and funky ♩ = 80

Here comes old flat-top, he come

groov-ing up slow-ly, he got   joo - joo eye-ball, he one

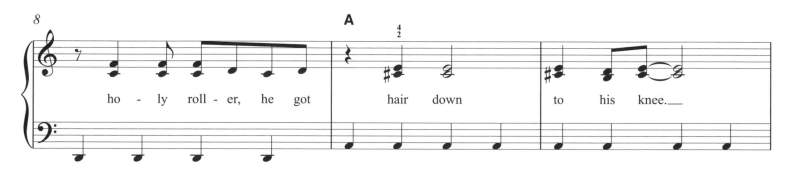

ho - ly roll-er, he got   hair down   to his knee.___

Got to be a jok - er, he just do what he please.___

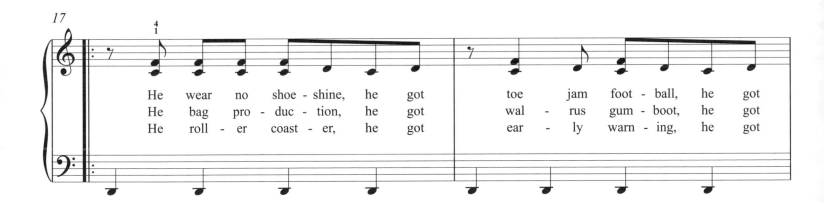

He wear no shoe - shine, he got   toe   jam foot - ball, he got
He bag pro - duc - tion, he got   wal - rus gum - boot, he got
He roll - er coast - er, he got   ear - ly warn - ing, he got

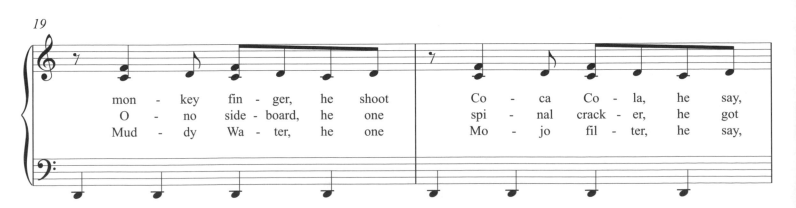

mon - key fin - ger, he shoot   Co - ca Co - la, he say,
O - no side - board, he one   spi - nal crack - er, he got
Mud - dy Wa - ter, he one   Mo - jo fil - ter, he say,

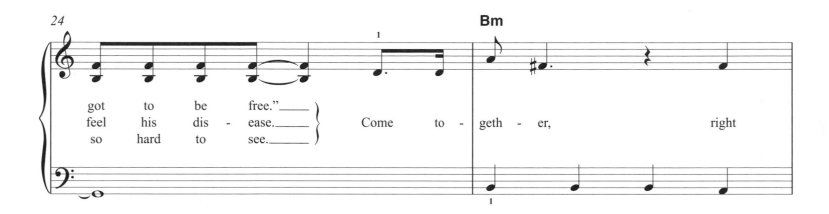

Can't Buy Me Love

Words and Music by John Lennon and Paul McCartney

Although Paul's lyric for this song is about not being able to buy love, Beatles fans certainly wanted to buy this record!
It holds the record for the highest number of advanced sales for a non-charity record – 1,400,000 singles in a single week!

Hints & Tips: Watch out for the B♭s and F♮s. They are quite unusual sounds in a piece in G major.

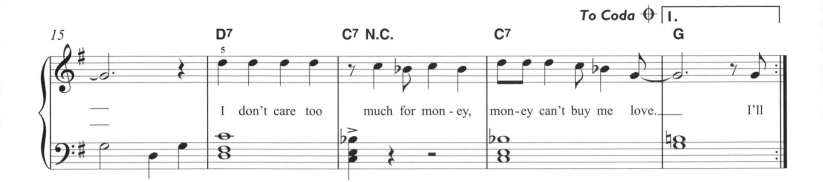

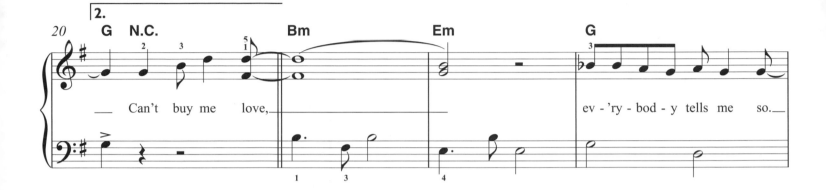

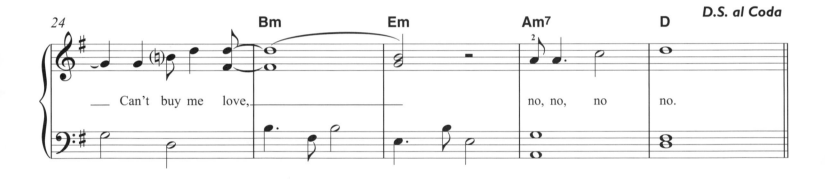

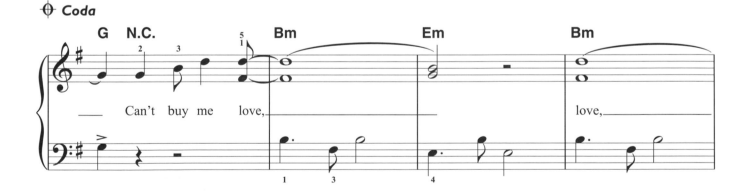

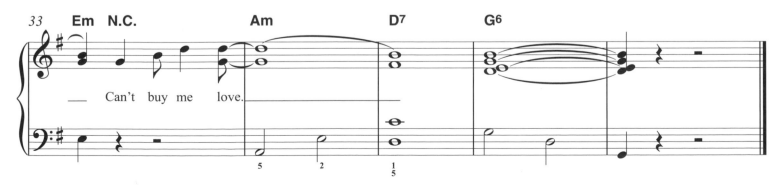

Blackbird

Words and Music by John Lennon and Paul McCartney

Upon hearing about the civil rights struggle in the USA, McCartney was inspired to write 'Blackbird'. He says of the song, "if it ever reached any of the people going through those problems, it might give them a little bit of hope". The song was composed shortly after the band's visit to Rishikesh in India and the signature guitar part is a favorite for budding players learning McCartney's fingerstyle technique.

Hints & Tips: The distinctive two-bar introduction in 'Blackbird' sets the mood and tempo. Carefully establish the crotchet (quarter note) beat first, as this song features plenty of changing note values. Just in the opening three bars you move from crotchets (quarter notes) to minims (half notes) to semiquavers (sixteenth notes). Be aware of accidentals too — practicing the hands separately can help you to identify these.

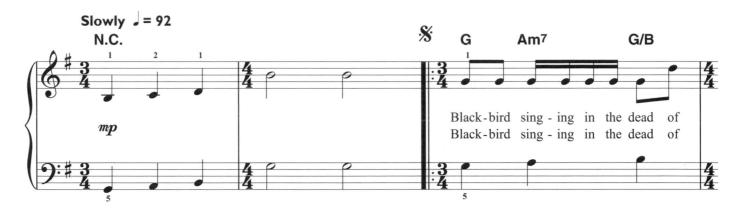

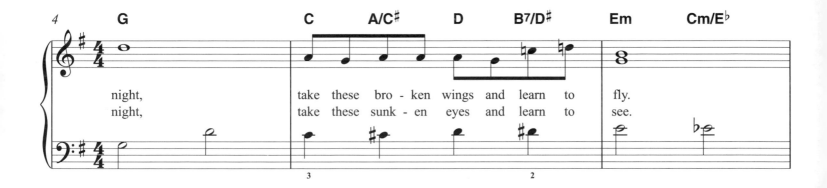

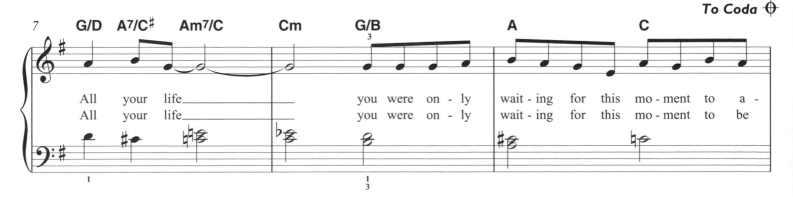

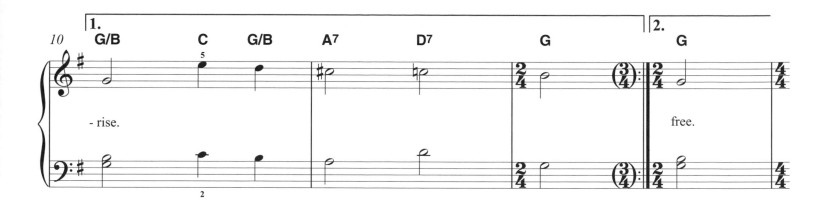

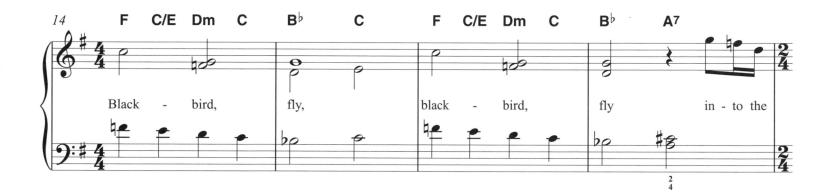

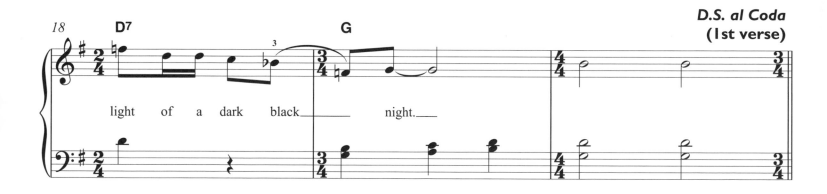

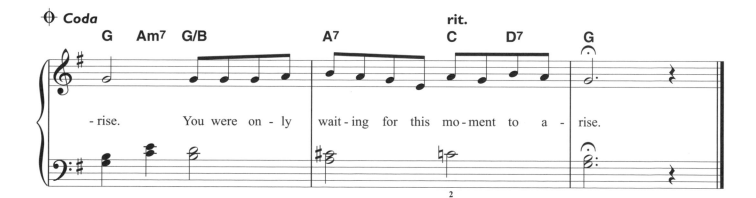

Day Tripper

Words and Music by John Lennon and Paul McCartney

The Beatles had received a streak of No. 1 hits by the time 'Day Tripper' was released as a double A-side with 'We Can Work It Out'. Around the time of this release, a TV special was aired about the band, called *The Music of Lennon & McCartney*, which interspersed mimed performances from The Beatles with appearances from other artists including Lulu and Cilla Black.

Hints & Tips: The hardest part of this is the left-hand riff right at the beginning.
It's all in the angle of your hand as you negotiate the sharps and flats. Try it slowly at first.

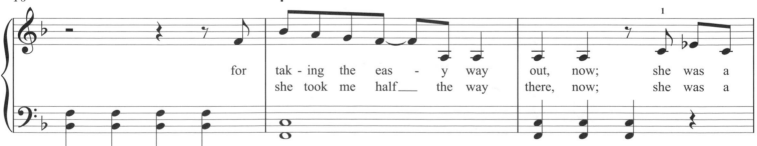

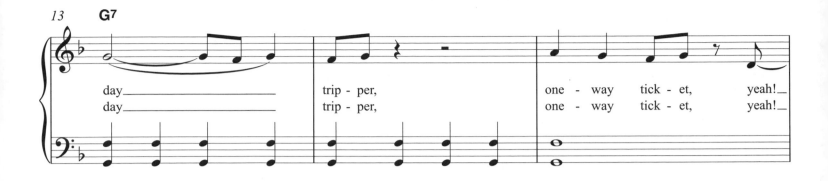

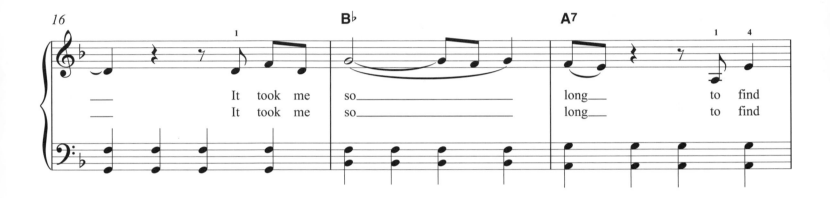

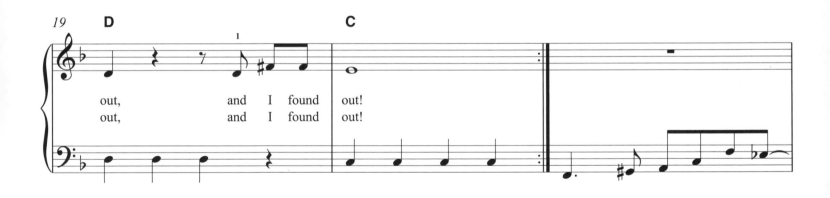

Eight Days a Week

Words and Music by John Lennon and Paul McCartney

This song didn't quite make the cut on numerous occasions! Originally written for the movie *Help!*, 'Eight Days a Week' ended up becoming part of the 1964 album, *Beatles for Sale*. Then, when on the cusp of being released as a single in the UK, it was dropped in favor of Lennon writing the smash hit 'I Feel Fine', which went straight to No. 1. Primarily written by McCartney, Lennon was not the biggest fan of the track and so it was never included in the band's live set.

**Hints & Tips: Take care with the right-hand dotted rhythms. You just need to feel
the beat underneath the rhythm. This could be played with a slight swing.**

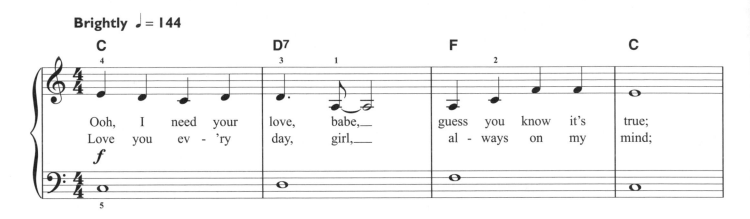

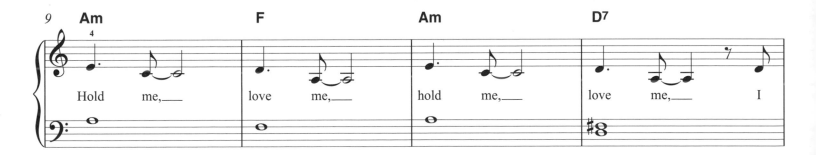

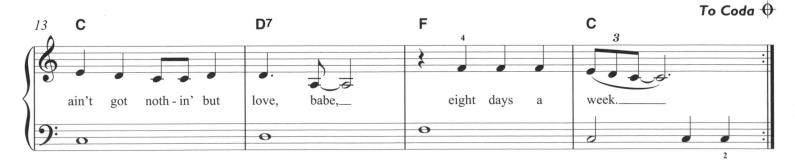

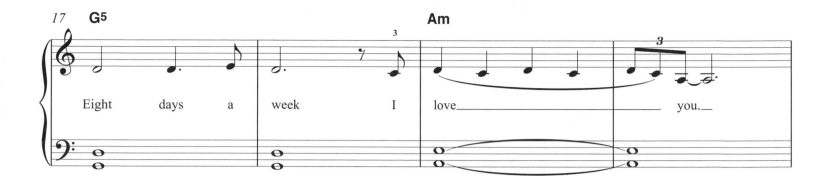

Eight days a week I love_____ you.___

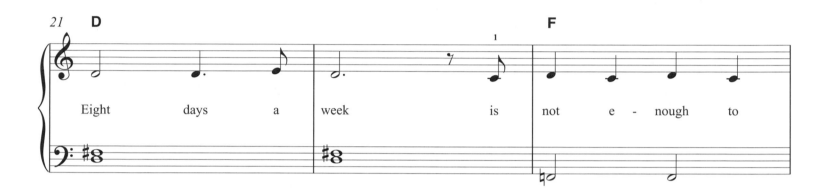

Eight days a week is not e - nough to

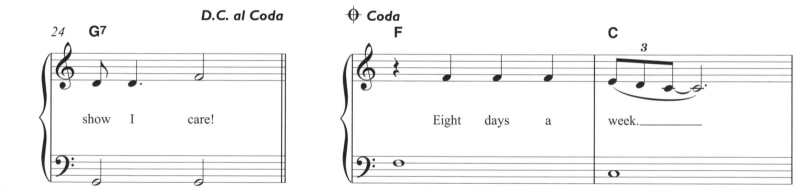

D.C. al Coda

$\oplus$ **Coda**

show I care!

Eight days a week._____

Eleanor Rigby

Words and Music by John Lennon and Paul McCartney

This is one of the few classics where none of the members played an instrument.
The producer George Martin arranged the song for a string ensemble at Paul's request.

Hints & Tips: Keep the left hand steady all the way through and aim not to play it too loudly.
Notice that your little finger and third finger in the left hand stay on the same notes all the way through!

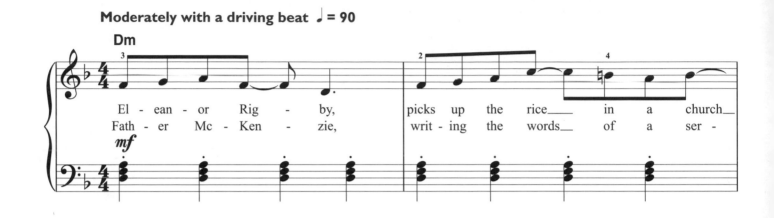

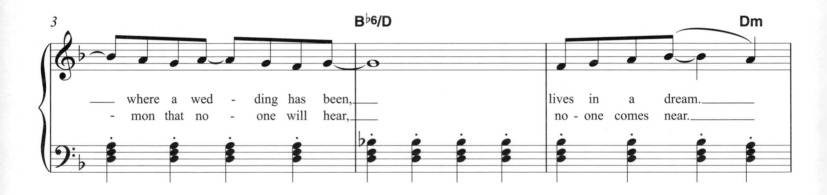

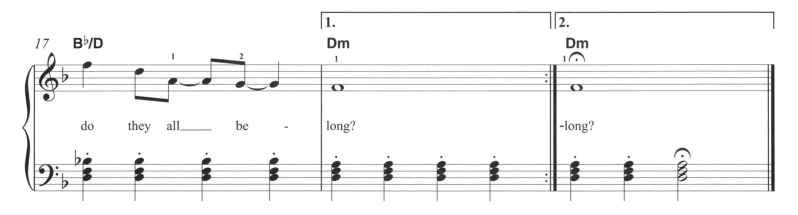

A Hard Day's Night

Words and Music by John Lennon and Paul McCartney

The title-single from the album of the same name, it hit the No. 1 spot in the UK on 23 July 1964.
A Hard Day's Night was also the band's first foray into feature-length film making
and rode on the wave of Beatlemania that had hit both sides of the Atlantic.

Hints & Tips: In the first half of bars 9 and 10 the left hand plays the same rhythm as the right hand.
Make sure that both hands play exactly together. The same happens in bars 29 and 30 also.

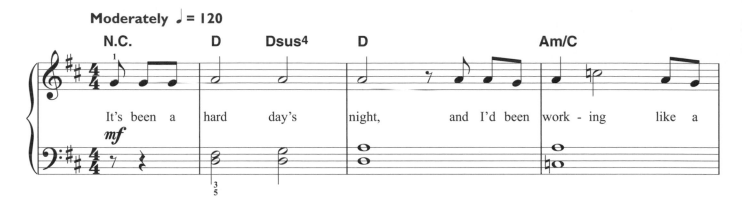

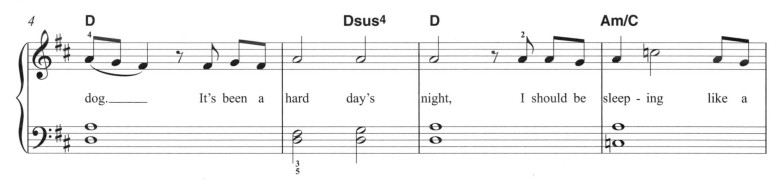

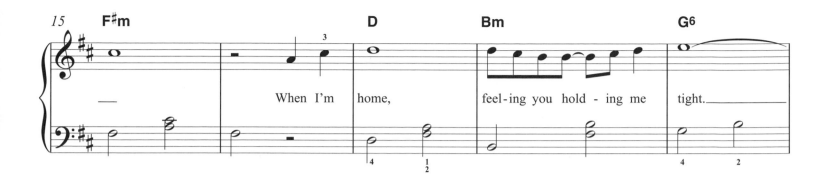

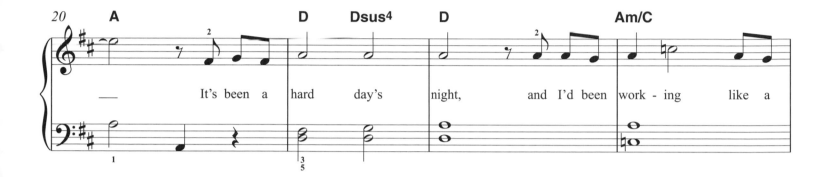

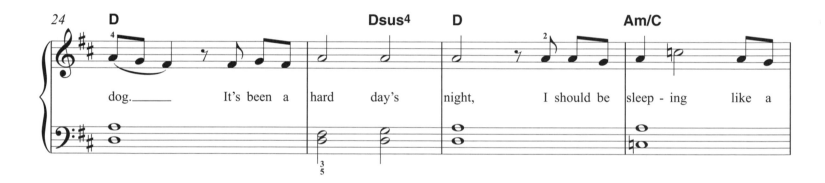

Hello, Goodbye

Words and Music by John Lennon and Paul McCartney

Coming from the band's 1967 album, *Magical Mystery Tour*, this song found its origins in a song writing experiment between Paul McCartney and friend Alistair Taylor. When Taylor asked Paul how he goes about writing a tune, Paul took him through a call and response exercise, where the pair shouted out opposite words to each other, which resulted in a call and response of 'Hello! Goodbye!' and the birth of the song, 'Hello, Goodbye'.

Hints & Tips: The right hand has some big stretches in this song, especially in the chorus. Keep the bridge of the hand high to negotiate the arpeggios. In bars 5–7 the left hand plays quavers (eighth notes) in a triad position. Keep these moving evenly.

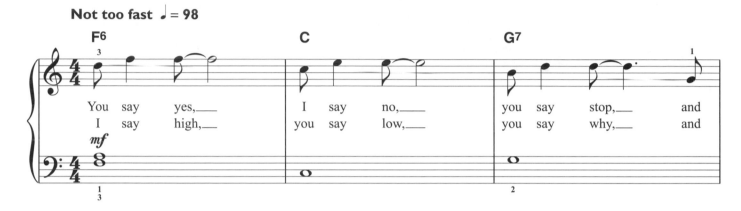

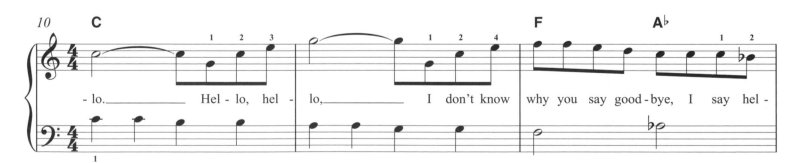

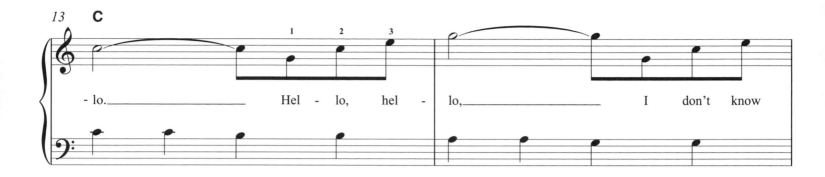

C

- lo._____ Hel - lo, hel - lo,_____ I don't know

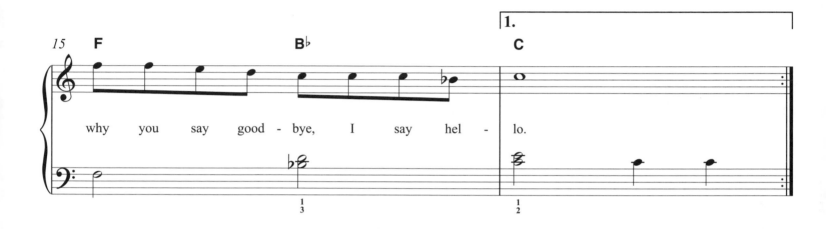

1.

F   **B♭**   **C**

why   you   say   good - bye,   I   say   hel - lo.

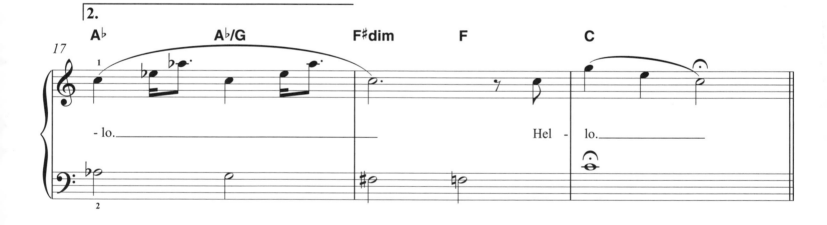

2.

A♭   **A♭/G**   **F♯dim**   **F**   **C**

- lo._____   Hel - lo._____

C/G   **C**

Hey - la,_____ he - ba,_ hel - lo - a...

Help!

Words and Music by John Lennon and Paul McCartney

Also the title of their second feature film, 'Help!' is considered to be the first Beatles song not written about love. The lyrics reflect the unrelenting pressure of fame that now bore down upon them. This would eventually lead to the band stopping playing live concerts altogether.

**Hints & Tips: Watch out for the tied notes in the melody.
If you sing the words as well, you may find it easier to get the rhythm right.**

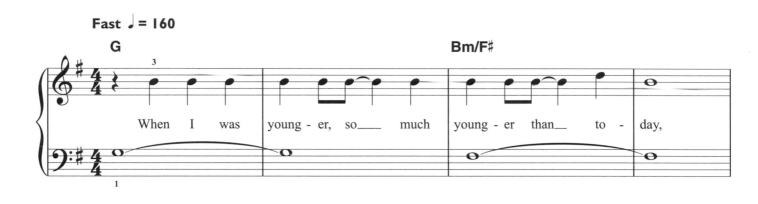

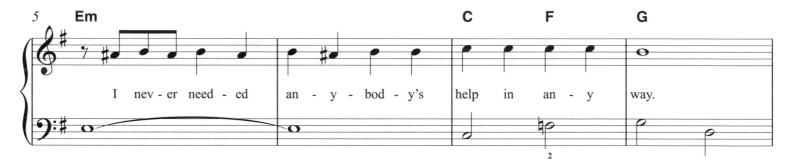

Help me if you can, I'm feel - ing down,_____ and I

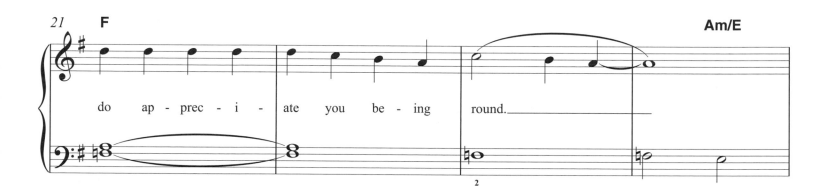

do ap - prec - i - ate you be - ing round._____

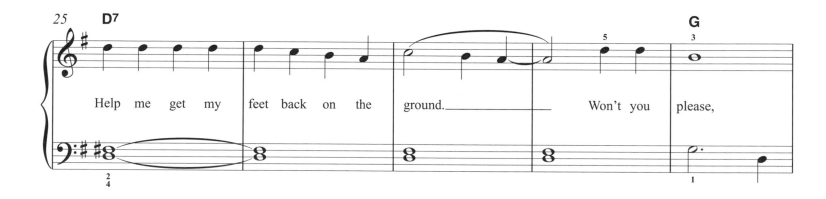

Help me get my feet back on the ground._____ Won't you please,

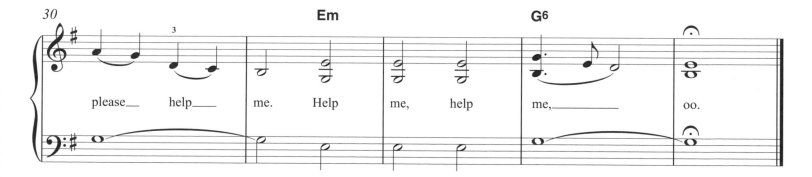

please___ help___ me. Help me, help me,_____ oo.

29

Here Comes the Sun

Words and Music by George Harrison

This is one of two songs on the *Abbey Road* album written by George Harrison – the other song being 'Something' which also features in this book. 'Here Comes the Sun' was written during a visit to his friend Eric Clapton's house, whilst walking in the garden and enjoying the sunshine.

Hints & Tips: Practice slowly enough to count the quavers (eighth notes), which always stay the same length. They may sound a little out of time when played with accents in bars 6—7, 21—22 and 30—31.

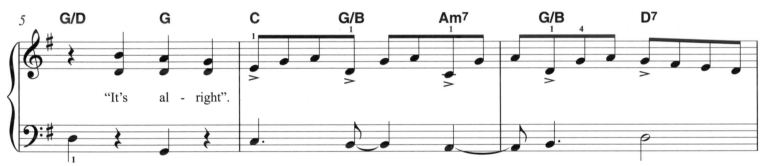

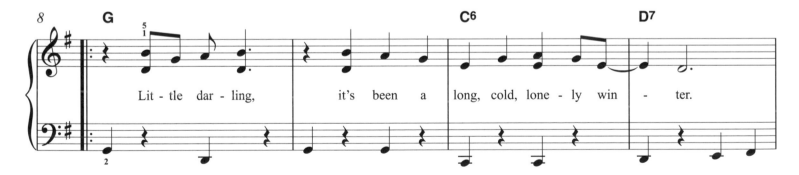

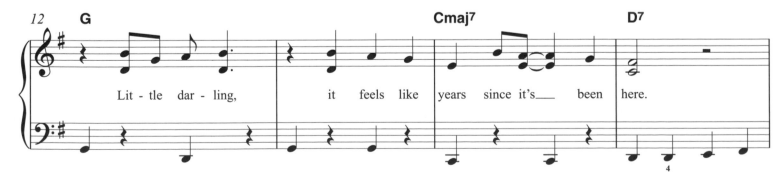

Here comes the sun. Here comes the sun, (and I say)

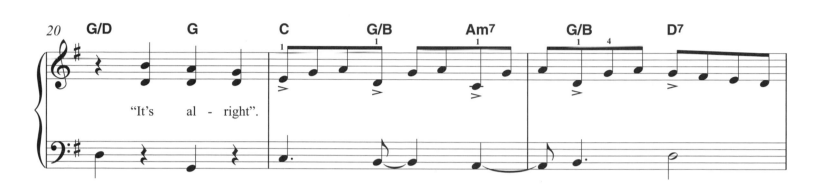

"It's al - right".

Here comes the sun.

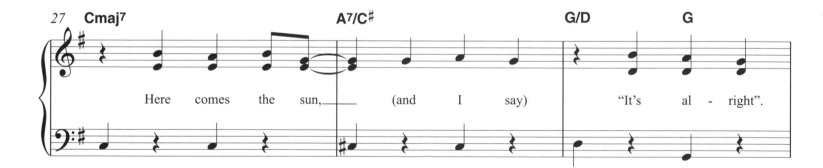

Here comes the sun, (and I say) "It's al - right".

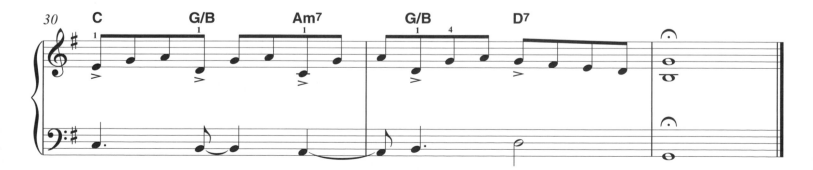

Here, There and Everywhere

Words and Music by John Lennon and Paul McCartney

Paul considered this his best love song, inspired by the Beach Boys song 'God Only Knows'
from their album *Pet Sounds,* which proved inspirational to the group. John Lennon even
held a copy as he walked into Abbey Road Studio to record 'Strawberry Fields Forever'.

Hints & Tips: Try to play with a rocking motion in the left hand. The melody is very
beautiful and jumps around quite a lot. Try to keep an even tone in spite of this.

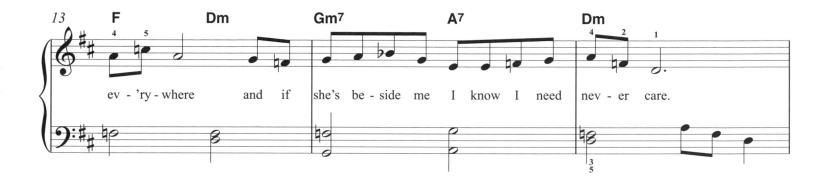

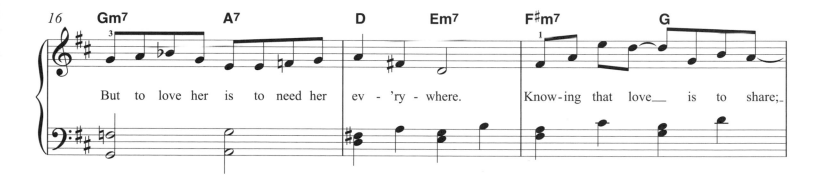

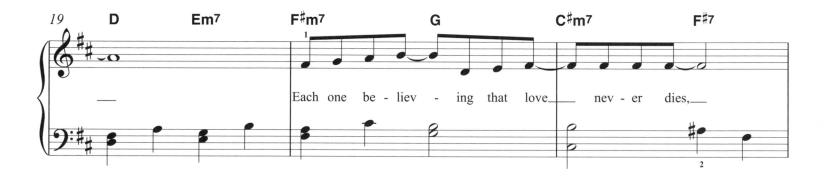

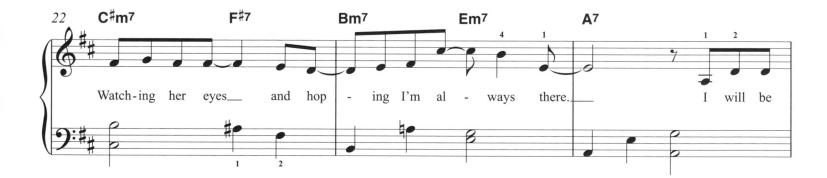

33

Hey Jude

Words and Music by John Lennon and Paul McCartney

Paul was inspired to pen this lyric to console John Lennon's son, Julian, but eventually decided to change the name. At the time it was the longest 45rpm single ever released, clocking in at 7 minutes, 11 seconds!

Hints & Tips: The left hand gives this piece its pulse so make sure you play it rhythmically and ensure all notes are held for their full durations. The middle section should be a little stronger and played with a fuller tone.

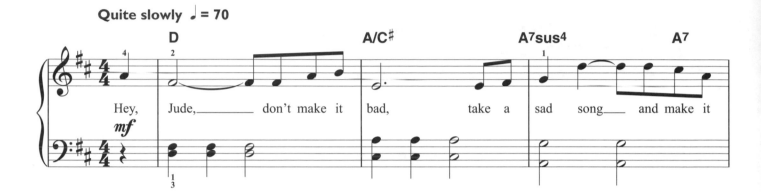

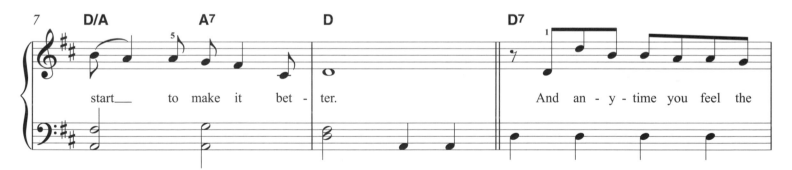

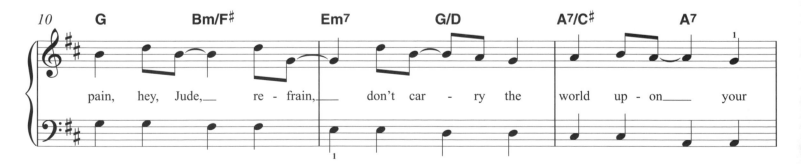

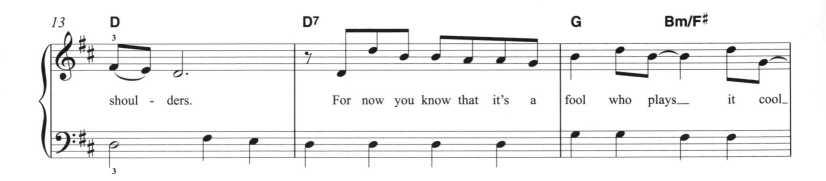

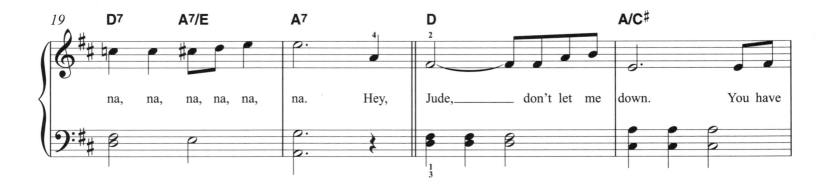

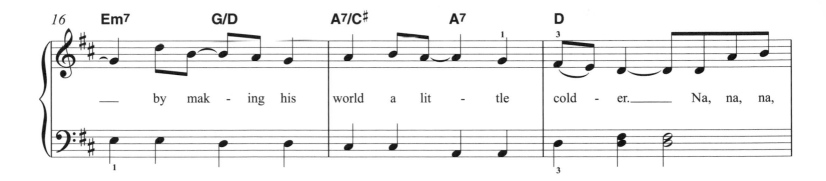

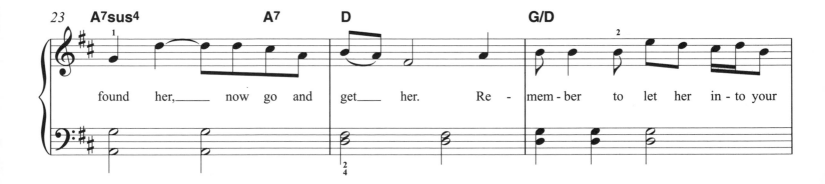

I Am the Walrus

Words and Music by John Lennon and Paul McCartney

This Lennon track was the B-side to McCartney's 'Hello, Goodbye', which irritated Lennon as he felt 'I Am the Walrus' was the stronger song. He purposefully wrote nonsense lyrics in the song to throw off members of the public who were looking for clues to confirm the rumor going around that one of The Beatles was dead! In a bizarre conspiracy, around this time, Paul McCartney was thought to have died in a car crash and replaced with a lookalike.

**Hints & Tips: The right hand has a lot of notes to play in this one.
Keep it steady and enjoy the wacky harmonies (and words!).**

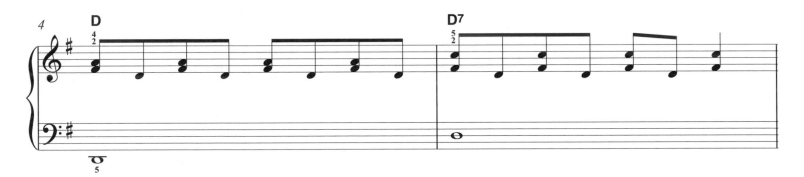

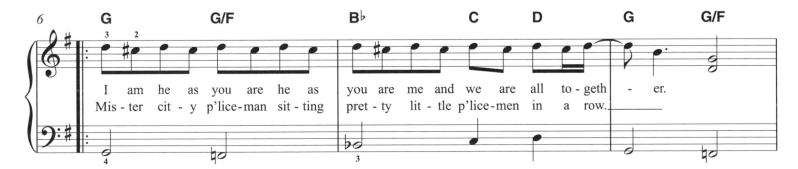

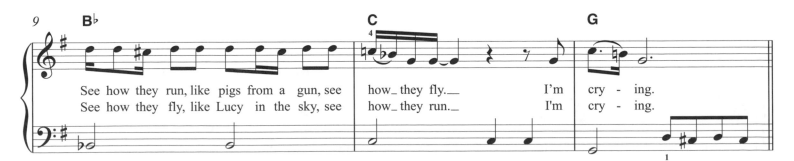

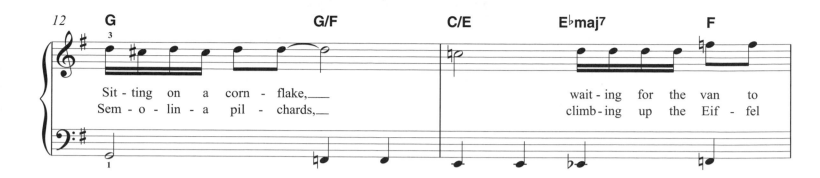

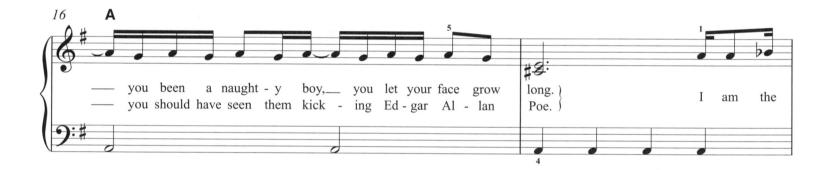

37

I Feel Fine

Words and Music by John Lennon and Paul McCartney

This was the 10th single and 6th No. 1 from The Beatles, who were by now well established in the UK and US charts. With the music video becoming a vital part of pop music promotion at this time, the group found themselves filming mimed performances for many of their hits. By the time 'I Feel Fine' came around, they were having more fun on set and we can even see Ringo riding a stationary bike instead of playing the drums in the video for this song!

Hints & Tips: This song should sound bright and happy. Take care with the big 7th stretch in the right hand — this is the well-known guitar riff.

Ba - by's good to me, you know,___ she's hap - py as can be, you know,___ she said so;
Ba - by says she's mine, you know,___ she tells me all the time, you know,___ she said so;
ba - by buys her things, you know,___ he buys her dia - mond rings, you know,___ she said so.

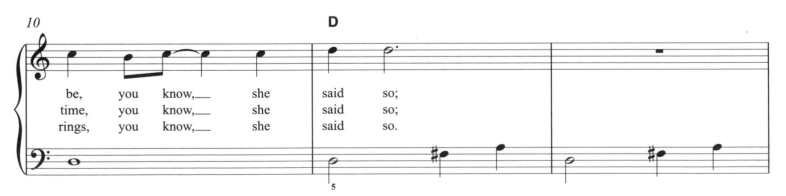

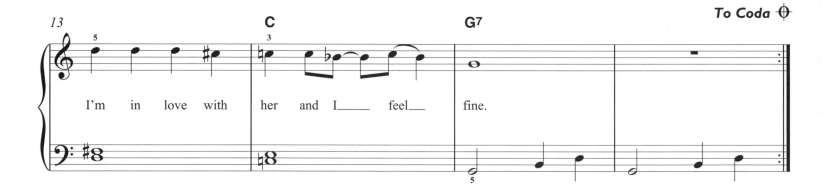

I'm in love with her and I____ feel__ fine.

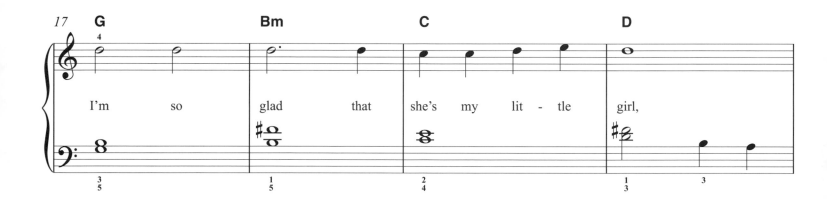

I'm so glad that she's my lit - tle girl,

D.S. al Coda

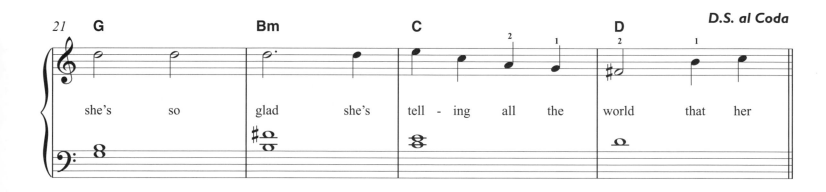

she's so glad she's tell - ing all the world that her

⊕ Coda

I Saw Her Standing There

Words and Music by John Lennon and Paul McCartney

This is one of the earlier Lennon-McCartney tracks written for the band, with the pair bunking off school one day in 1962 in order to start putting it together. This was a popular hit in their live set in Liverpool at the band's favorite haunt, The Cavern Club. 'I Saw Her Standing There' became part of the *Please Please Me* album, which was released in 1963, and was one of ten album tracks recorded in just one day!

Hints & Tips: The left hand is quite busy in this song, playing notes on almost every beat. The right hand bounces off this steady pulse in places like bars 5 and 7.

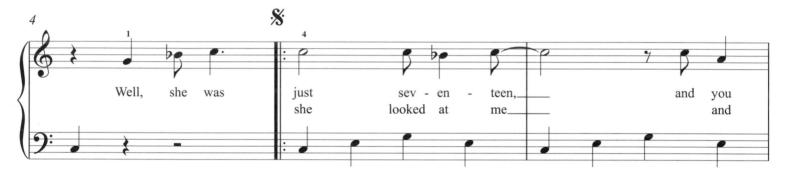

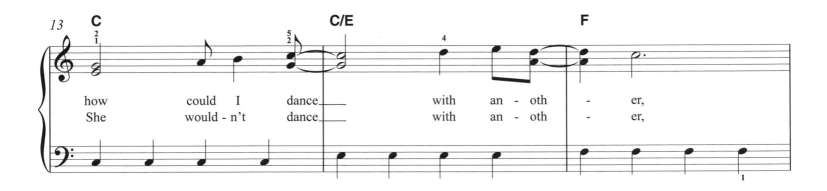

how   could   I   dance___   with   an - oth   - er,

She   would-n't   dance__   with   an - oth   - er,

woo,   when   I   saw   her   stand - -   ing

woo,   when   I   saw   her   stand - -   ing

To Coda ⊕

there?   Well,

there.   Well,   my

heart   went   boom__   when   I   crossed   that   room,

and I held her hand in

mine, mine.

Oh, we

Oh, since I saw her

stand - - ing there.

I Want to Hold Your Hand

Words and Music by John Lennon and Paul McCartney

'I Want to Hold Your Hand' was The Beatles' best-selling single
worldwide, released on the *Meet the Beatles* album in 1963.

Hints & Tips: Be careful when placing harmonies in the right hand. Especially when
they fall on an offbeat, be careful to sound the notes at exactly the same time.

With a steady Rock beat ♩ = 120

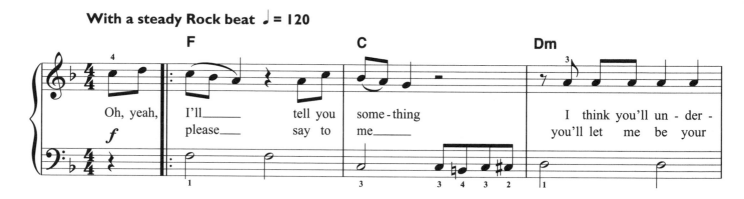

Oh, yeah,   I'll___ tell you some-thing   I think you'll un-der-
please___ say to me___   you'll let me be your

-stand.   When   I___ say that some-thing,
man.   And   please___ say to me___

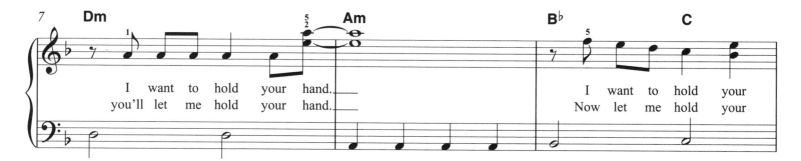

I want to hold your hand.___   I want to hold your
you'll let me hold your hand.___   Now let me hold your

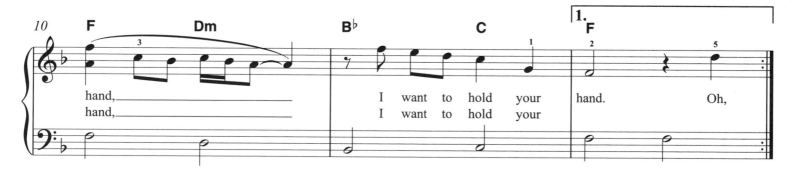

hand,___   I want to hold your hand.   Oh,
hand,___   I want to hold your

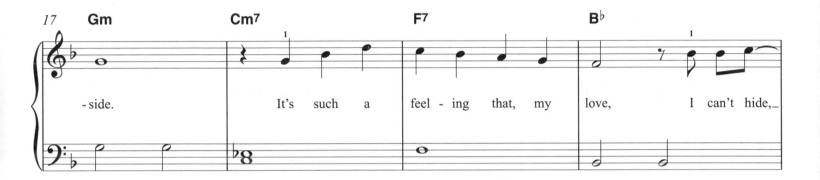

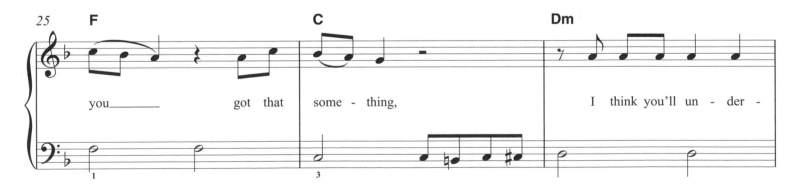

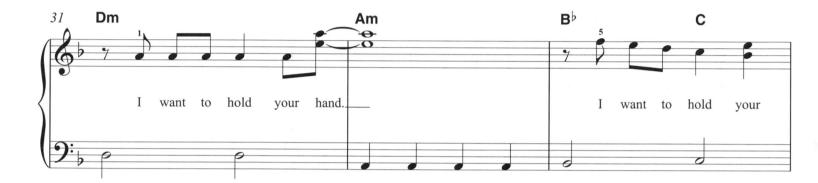

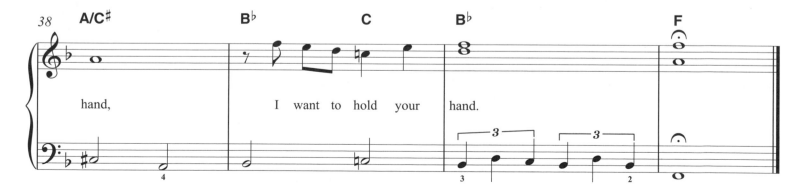

In My Life

Words and Music by John Lennon and Paul McCartney

From the 1965 album, *Rubber Soul*, John's inspired lyric remembering his childhood and upbringing has become an unofficial epitaph for the songwriter since his death in 1980. The laid-back style is offset by a keyboard solo in a baroque style.

Hints & Tips: There are baroque decorations in the melody itself, e.g. bars 3 and 7. Try to play these bars with exceptional elegance and poise. The slurs in bars 9 and 13 are important as they represent a change in character. Play them very smoothly, almost as if your hands are glued to the keyboard!

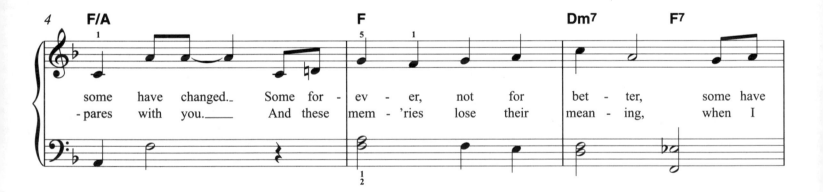

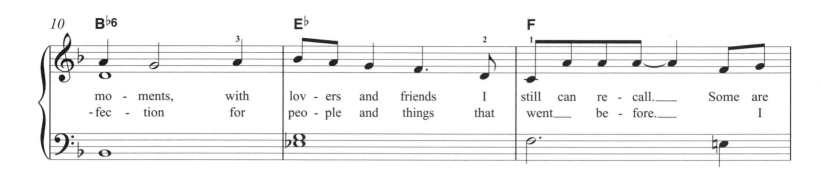

moments, with lov - ers and friends I still can re - call.___ Some are
-fec - tion with for peo - ple and things that went___ be - fore.___ I

dead___ and___ some___ are___ liv - ing, in my_____ life, I've
know I'll of - ten stop and think a - bout them, in my_____ life, I'll

To Coda ⊕ | **1.**

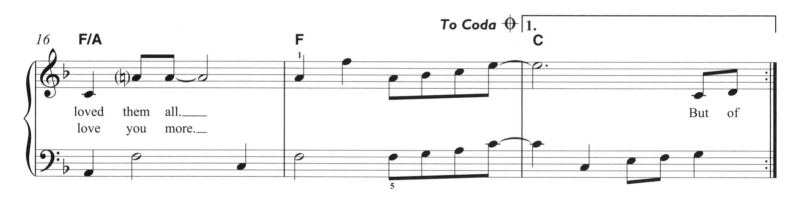

loved them all.___
love you more.___ But of

2.

D.S. al Coda   ⊕ **Coda**

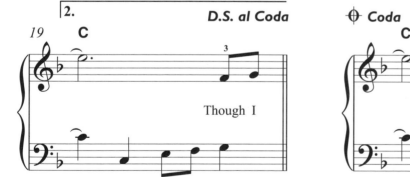

Though I

In my_____ life, I'll

love you more.__

Lady Madonna

Words and Music by John Lennon and Paul McCartney

Supposedly inspired by a Humphrey Lyttleton jazz classic 'Bad Penny Blues', 'Lady Madonna' went to No. 1 on the 27th March 1968 and was the band's 14th No. 1 hit. It features the group blowing through cupped hands to imitate a brass section.

Hints & Tips: This piece should be rhythmically sharp throughout. Pay special attention to the staccato dots; the left hand in bars 23 and 24 is a good example. Try to make the staccato notes as short as possible to distinguish them from the other, longer notes.

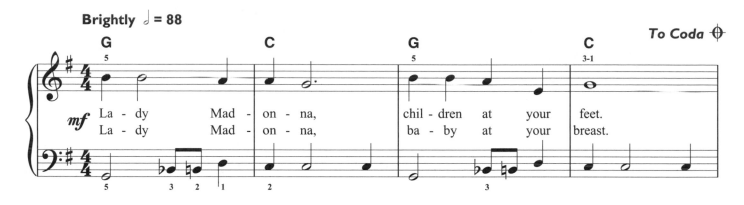

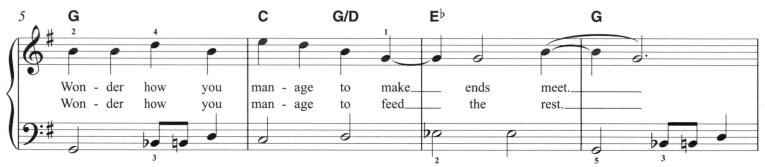

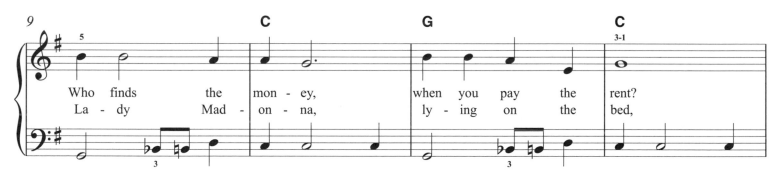

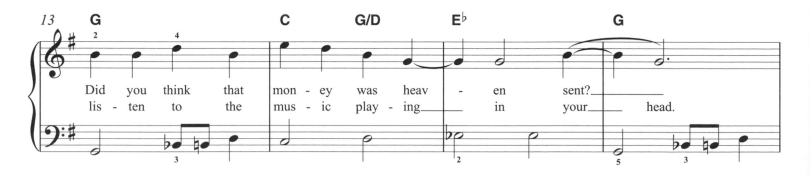

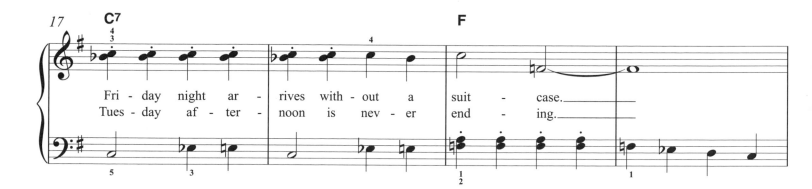

Fri - day night ar - rives with - out a suit - case.
Tues - day af - ter - noon is nev - er end - ing.

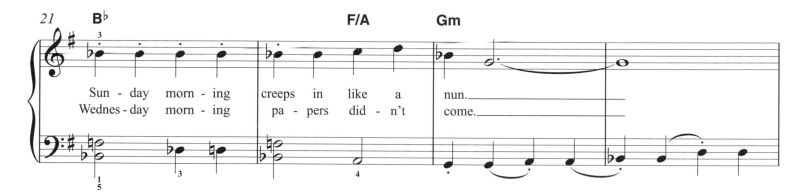

Sun - day morn - ing creeps in like a nun.
Wednes - day morn - ing pa - pers did - n't come.

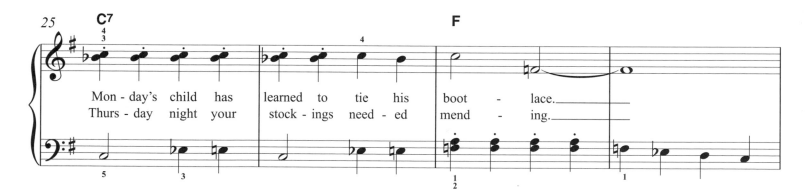

Mon - day's child has learned to tie his boot - lace.
Thurs - day night your stock - ings need - ed mend - ing.

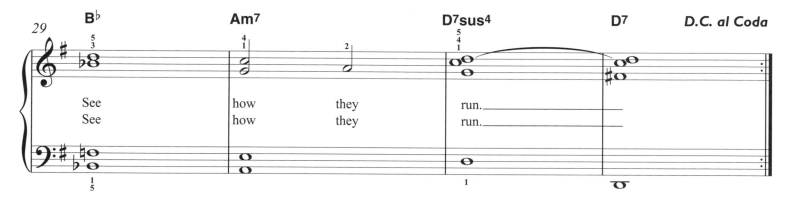

See how they run.
See how they run.

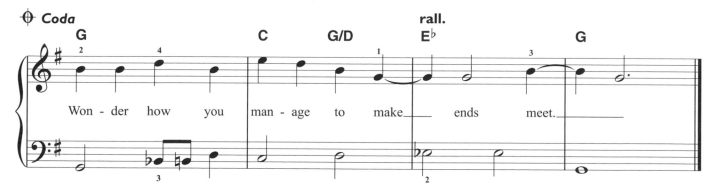

Won - der how you man - age to make ends meet.

49

Let It Be

Words and Music by John Lennon and Paul McCartney

The last Beatles single to be released, 'Let It Be' was issued on 6 March 1970. It is one of a few Beatles songs that exist in multiple authorized versions. It was thought to be a plea for the group to make their peace with each other as they started their solo careers.

Hints & Tips: This piece has an almost hymn-like quality. Try to play it with appropriate solemnity. Play the more complex rhythms in a more relaxed and unperturbed way.

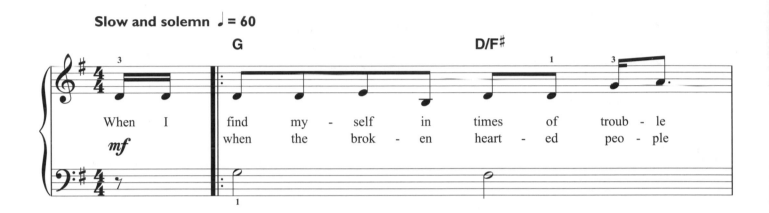

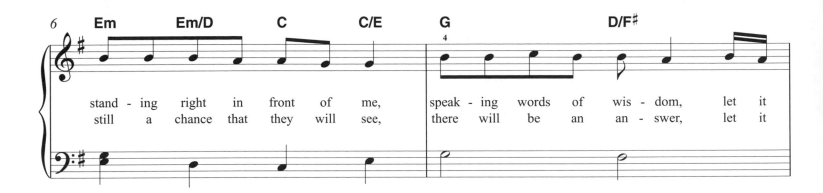

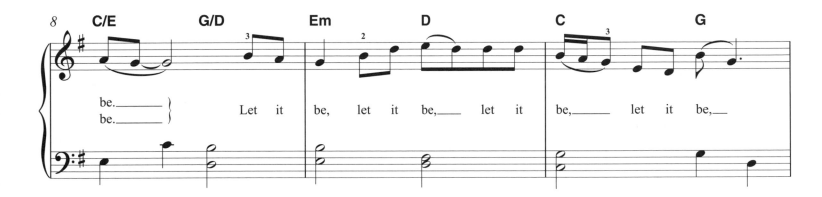

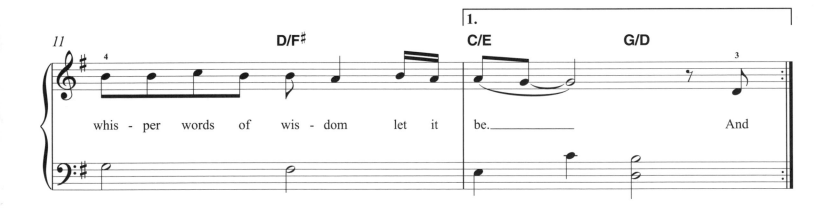

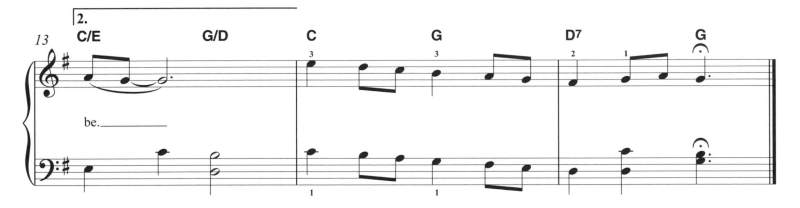

The Long and Winding Road

Words and Music by John Lennon and Paul McCartney

This song was written by McCartney in 1969 at a difficult time for the band, who broke up officially in April of the following year. Tensions were high between the members, which led to producer Phil Spector working on this track without the band's input. In production, he removed Harrison and Ringo's parts and added other instrumentation to the song, which resulted in an entirely different sound than McCartney had envisioned. This led to McCartney attempting to ban its release, which he managed in the UK but could not stop the single dropping in the USA.

Hints & Tips: This song is slow and grand, but has an elegant simplicity.
Keep it gentle, apart from the chords in bars 3 and 4, and the ending.

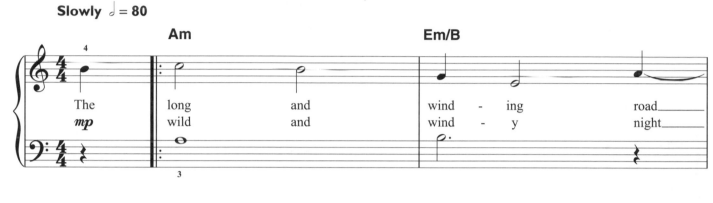

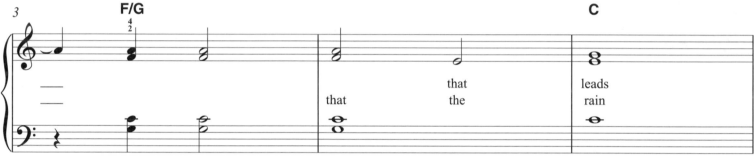

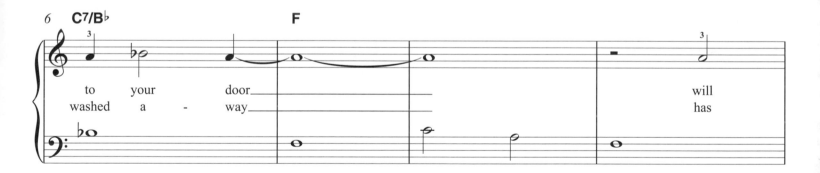

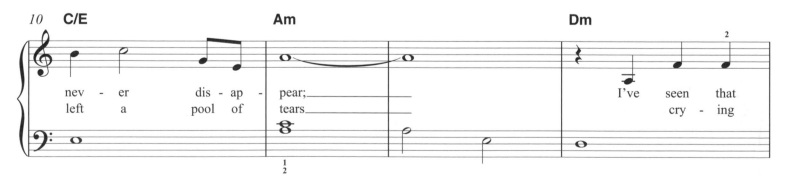

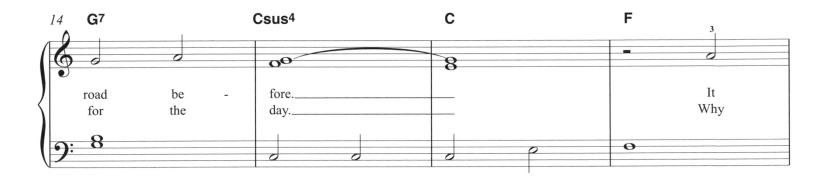

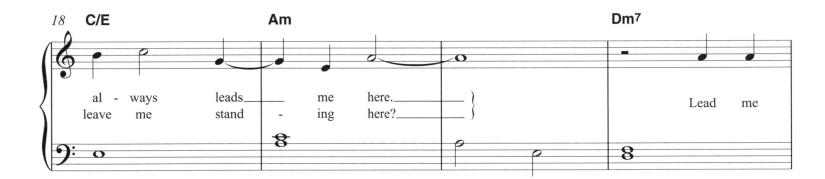

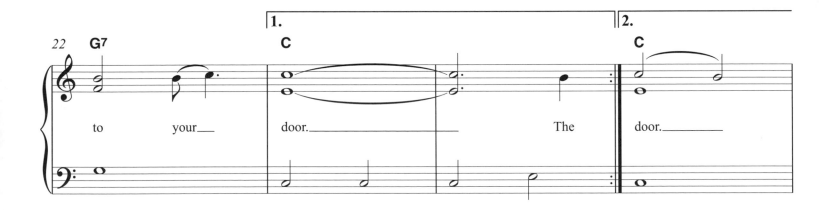

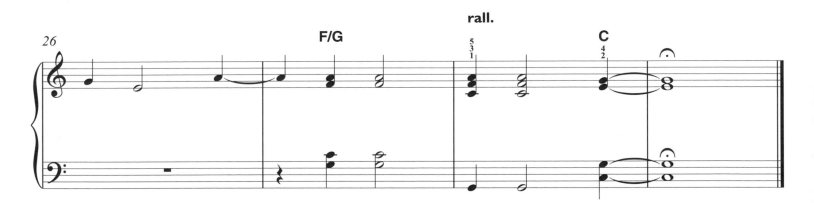

Love Me Do

Words and Music by John Lennon and Paul McCartney

'Love Me Do' was The Beatles' debut single in 1962. The song was an early Lennon-McCartney composition from 1958, although it wouldn't be recorded by the group for another four years.

Hints & Tips: The first eight bars mimic the opening harmonica solo on the recording. You'll need only two chords, G7 and C (or C/D), until the middle eight bars when the D chord joins in. Note the slanted lines moving from treble to bass and back to treble clef. This shows where the melody moves from hand to hand.

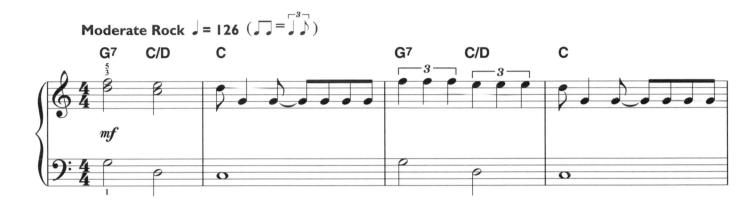

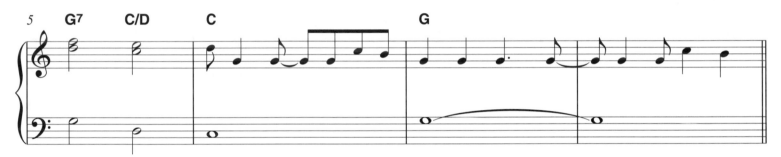

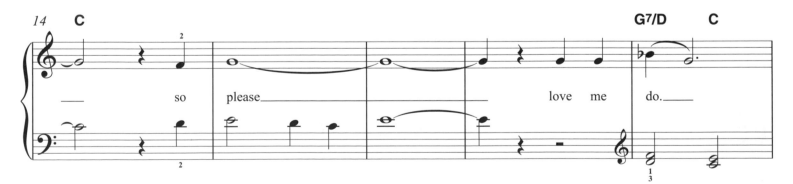

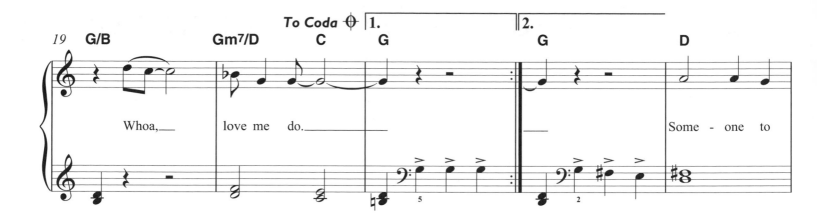

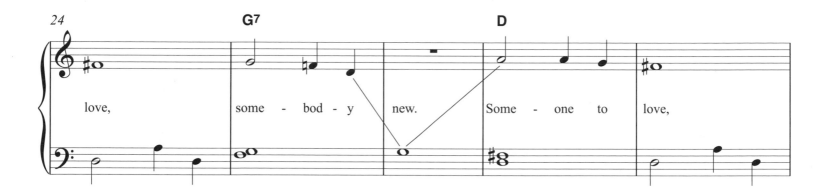

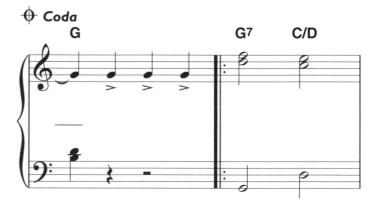

Lucy in the Sky With Diamonds

Words and Music by John Lennon and Paul McCartney

Another song inspired by Julian, John's son. This time Julian had painted a picture which he then showed
to his father. When asked what the picture depicted, Julian replied "it's Lucy in the sky with diamonds!"

Hints & Tips: Try playing the first eight bars an octave higher for a bell-like effect. Watch out
for the two key signature changes, and for the change of time and tempo (speed) at bar 36.

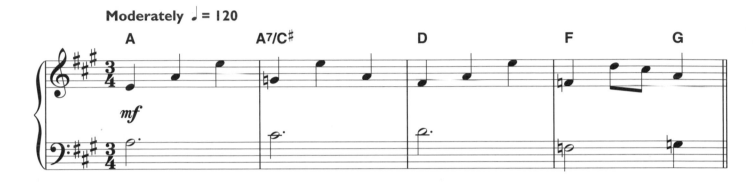

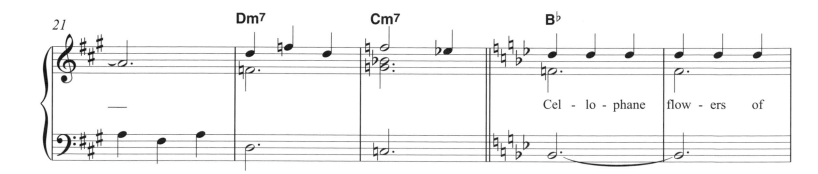

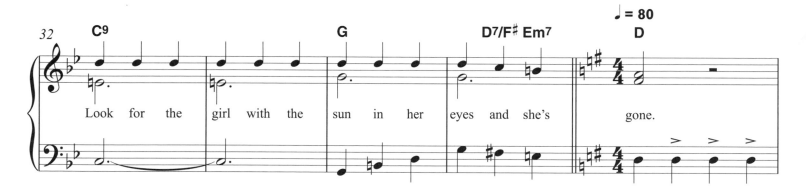

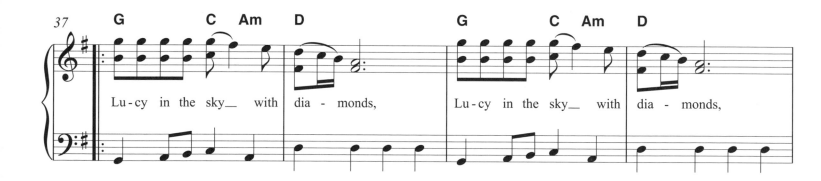

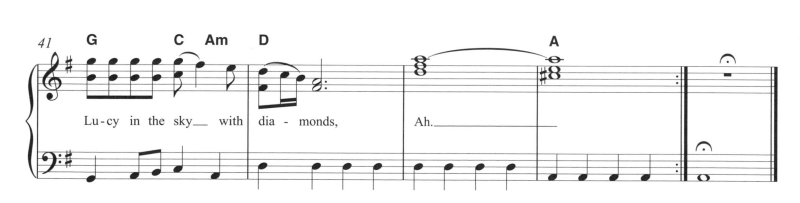

Ob-La-Di, Ob-La-Da

Words and Music by John Lennon and Paul McCartney

The phrase, 'ob-la-di, ob-la-da' was a phrase used by Nigerian conga player and friend of McCartney, Jimmy Scott. McCartney had originally wanted to record the song as a ballad, but after more than 50 takes of this, Lennon had had enough and took over the piano part, creating the upbeat version we hear on *The White Album* of 1968.

Hints & Tips: The crotchet pulse is quite fast in this song. It might pay to play the left hand through a few times on its own first to get the hang of the accompaniment. The arrangement is in C so it's nearly all white notes.

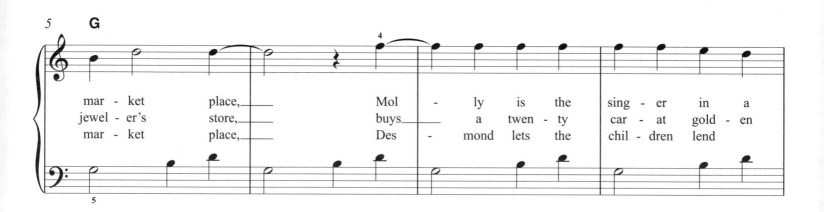

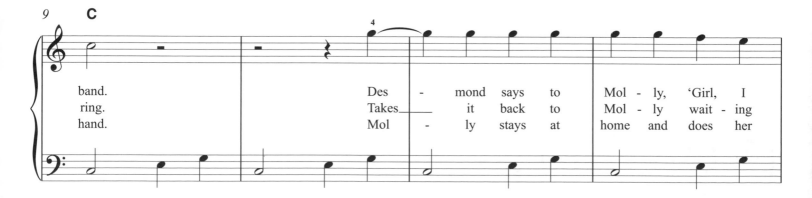

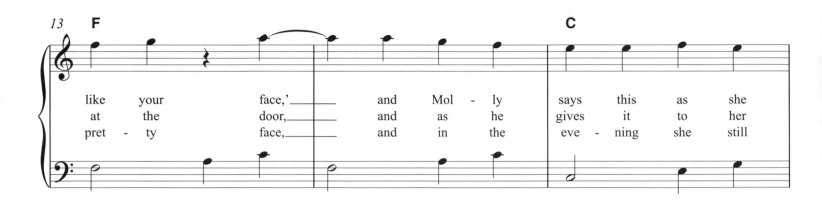

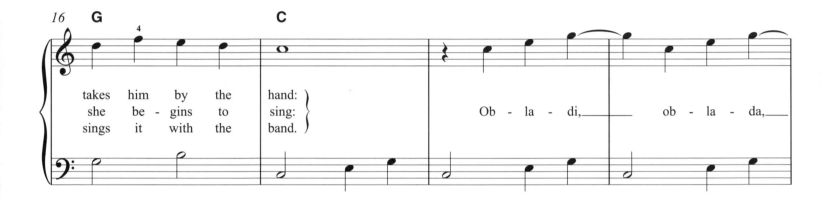

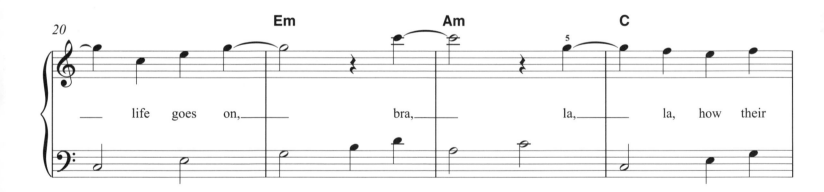

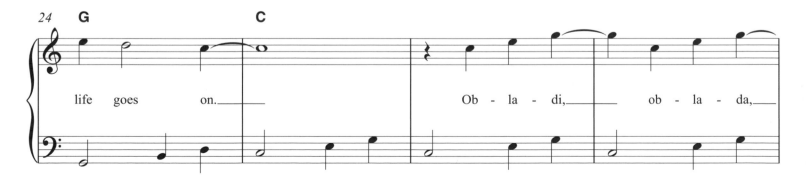

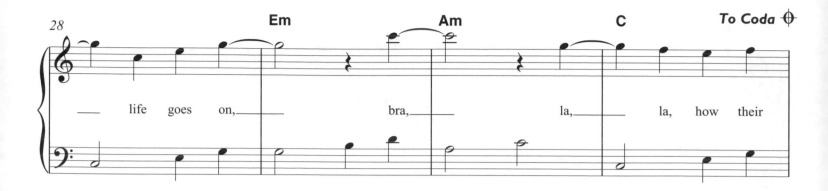

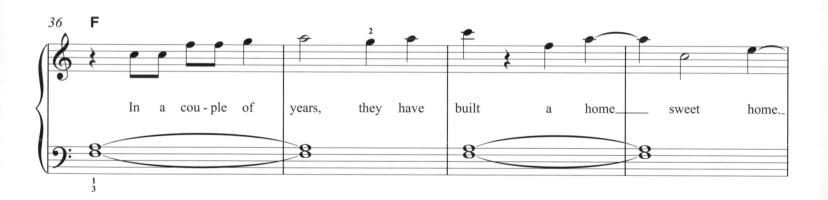

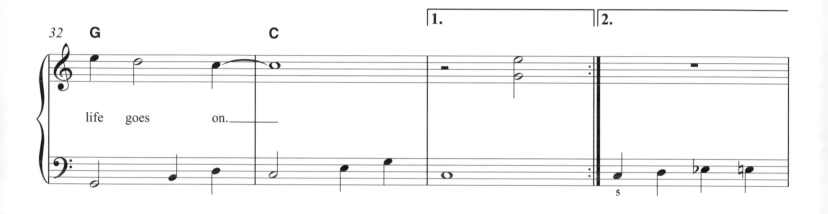

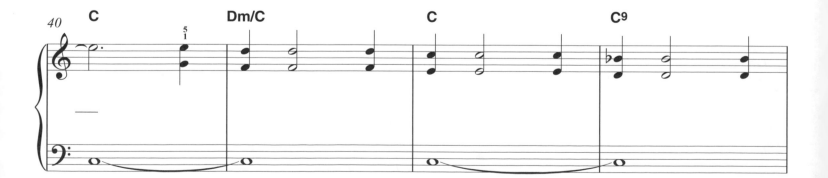

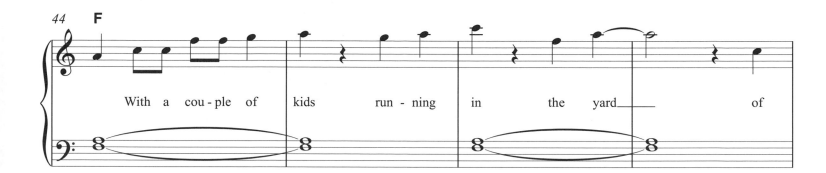

With a cou-ple of kids run-ning in the yard___ of

D.S. al Coda

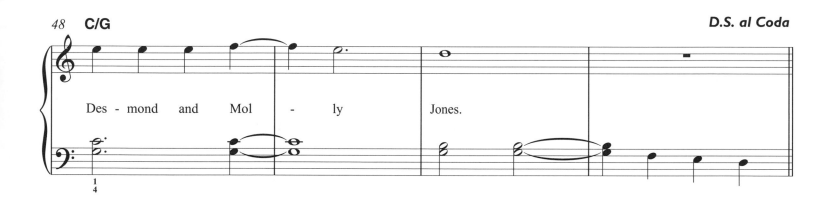

Des - mond and Mol - ly Jones.

Coda

life goes on.___ And if you

want some fun,___ take ob - la - di - bla - da.

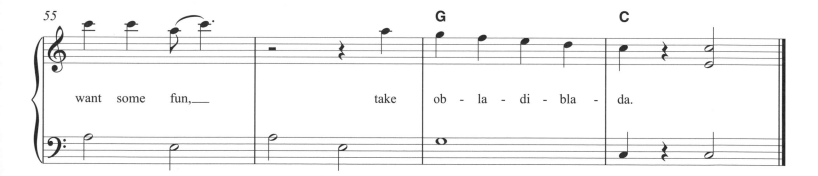

Penny Lane

Words and Music by John Lennon and Paul McCartney

Named after a place in Liverpool, this song contains a piccolo trumpet solo. McCartney was inspired after hearing trumpeter David Mason's performance of one of Bach's Brandenburg Concertos.

Hints & Tips: Notice that, in bar 15, the melody dips into the left hand. It is important that the transition is seamless. Try to play the 'walking bass' at the beginning with a solid, rolling feel.

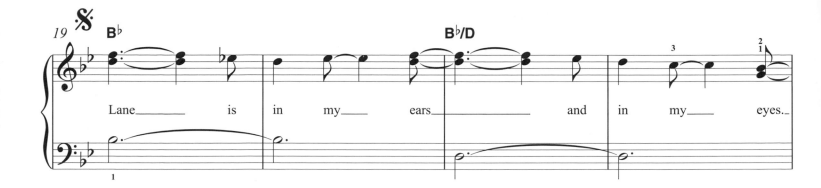

Lane_____ is in my____ ears_____ and in my____ eyes.__

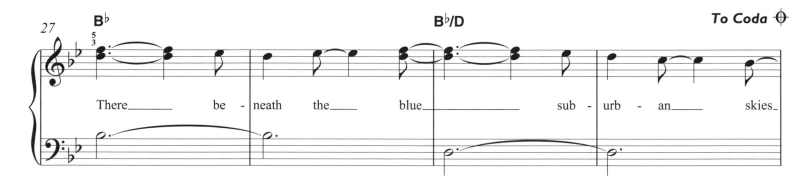

There_____ be - neath the____ blue_____ sub - urb - an____ skies_

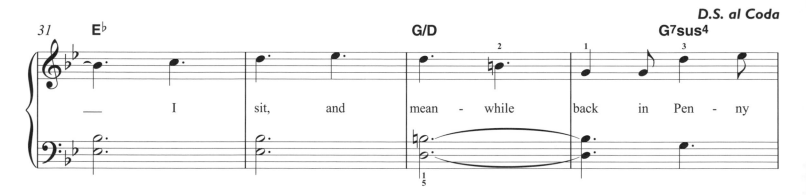

D.S. al Coda

____ I sit, and mean - while back in Pen - ny

⊕ Coda

Please Please Me

Words and Music by John Lennon and Paul McCartney

Known for their squeaky-clean image in the early years, The Beatles did not comment on the potential innuendo of the lyrics for 'Please Please Me', part of their 1963 album of the same name. This track very nearly became their first official No. 1, but it was their next single, 'From Me to You', that ended up topping the charts for the first time. The band were influenced by Bing Crosby's song 'Please', which includes the lyric "Oh please, lend your little ear to my pleas".

Hints & Tips: Take care with the left-hand repeated notes in bar 6. Also watch the dotted rhythm in bars 11—14, shared by both hands. This is known as a syncopation; lean on the off-beat note.

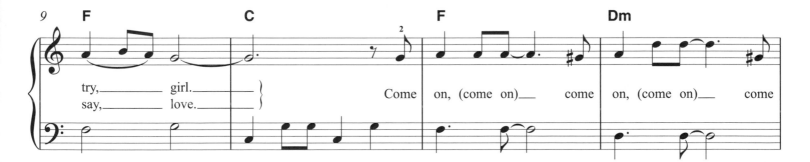

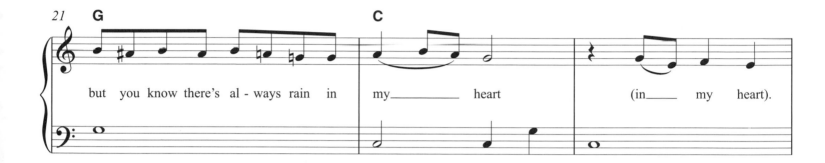

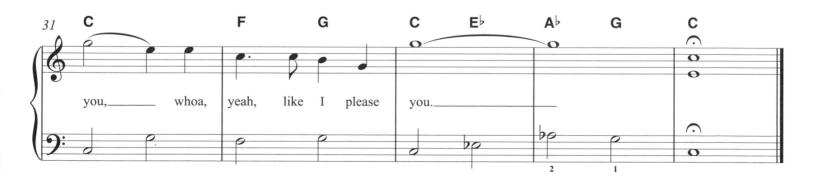

Paperback Writer

Words and Music by John Lennon and Paul McCartney

After receiving grief from an aunt about only writing love songs, McCartney was inspired to write 'Paperback Writer' after helping friends to set up the Indica Bookshop in 1966. It became the band's first No. 1 hit that wasn't about love! However, it did lead to the beginning of a love story for one band member, as the Indica gallery was where Lennon met Yoko Ono for the first time. Their relationship became a huge controversy, particularly due to the speculation of Ono's involvement in the eventual break-up of the band four years later.

**Hints & Tips: Try this hands separately first, as both hands have a lot of notes to play.
Choose a reasonable tempo so that the quavers (eighth notes) aren't too quick.**

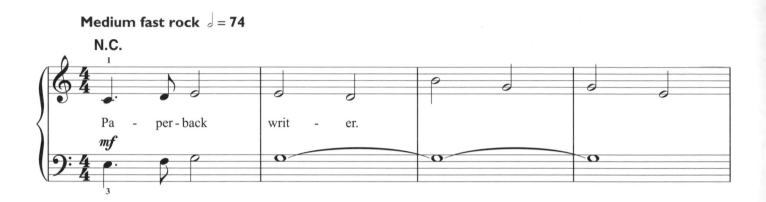

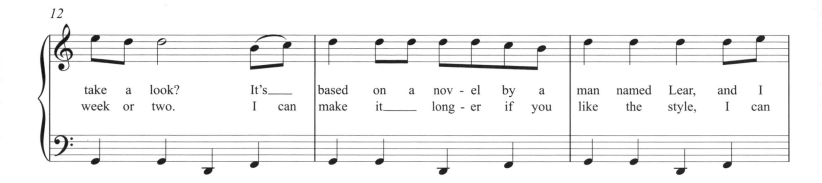

take a look? It's___ based on a nov-el by a man named Lear, and I
week or two. I can make it___ long-er if you like the style, I can

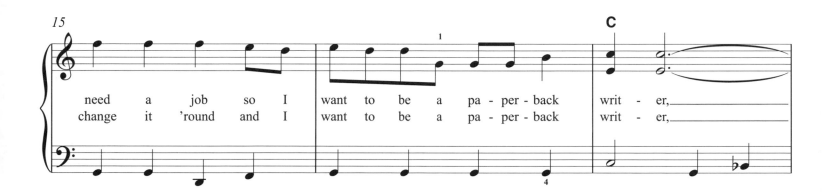

need a job so I want to be a pa-per-back writ - er,___
change it 'round and I want to be a pa-per-back writ - er,___

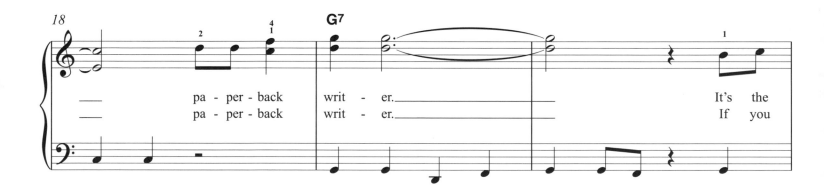

___ pa-per-back writ - er.___ It's the
___ pa-per-back writ - er.___ If you

dirt - y sto-ry of a dirt - y man,___ and his cling - ing wife does-n't
real - ly like it you can have the right,___ it could make a mil - lion for you

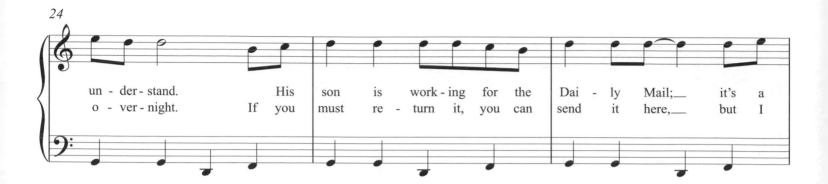

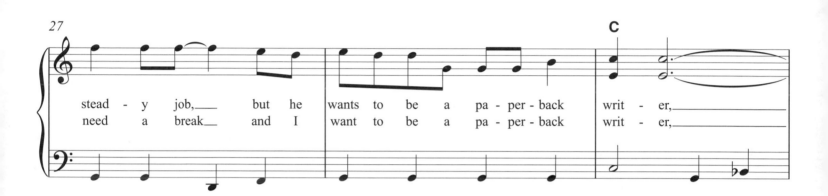

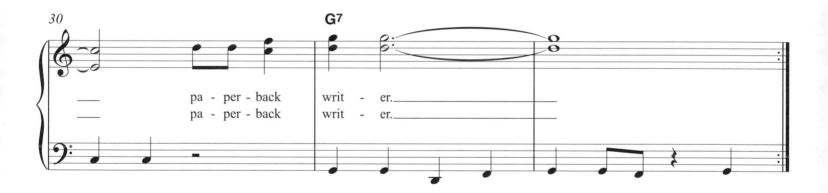

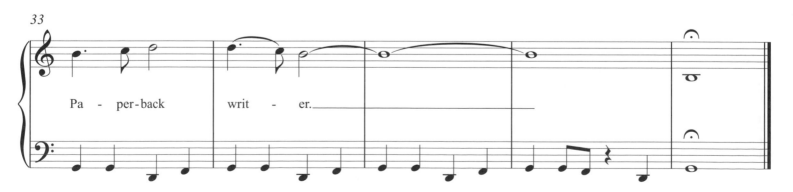

Revolution

Words and Music by John Lennon and Paul McCartney

Lennon and McCartney fought between which of their songs – Lennon's 'Revolution' or McCartney's 'Hey Jude' – would get the A-side of the proposed single release in 1968. McCartney won out, giving the group another No. 1 hit. However, Lennon's 'Revolution' was considered a refreshing departure from their pop-rock image, with an iconic guitar sound that was so distorted, some customers tried to return their 45 RPM as they thought it was faulty!

Hints & Tips: Have a quick listen to this song before playing to get the sense of the swing rhythm. There are also a lot of triplets to play in the right hand. Be sure to count carefully: the song is in 4/4 but there are some 2/4 bars.

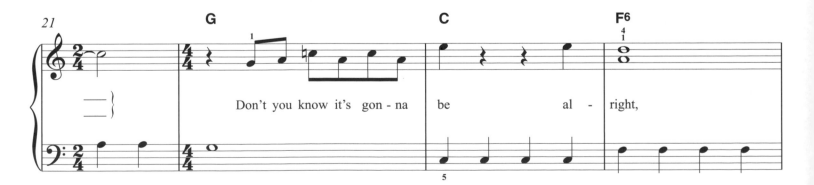

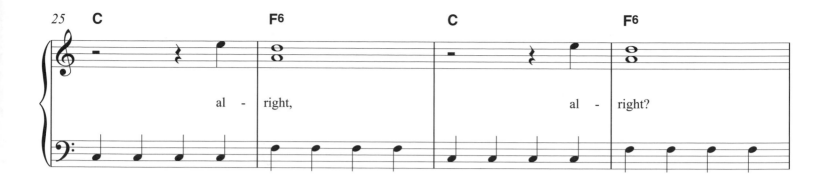

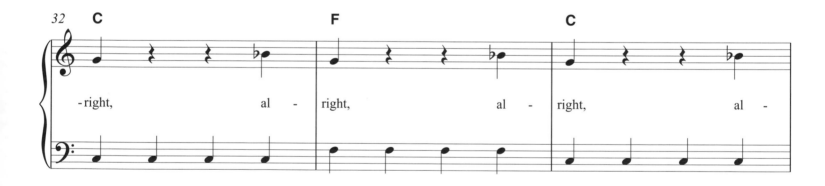

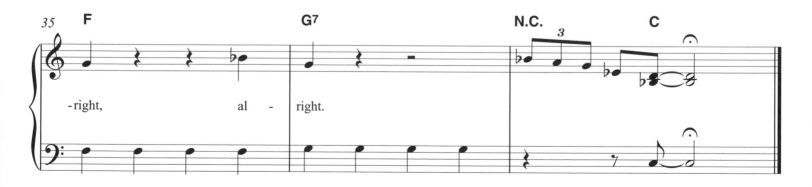

She Loves You

Words and Music by John Lennon and Paul McCartney

This single quickly came to epitomize the phenomenon of Beatlemania, with the Fab Four being hounded and harassed wherever they went by gangs of screaming hysterical fans. The song also coined the catchphrase "yeah, yeah, yeah!" and spent six weeks at the top of the UK charts.

Hints & Tips: The chord in bars 13, 14, 21 and 29 is quite shocking in a piece such as this. Make sure you've spotted the E♭s and play them with a level of drama!

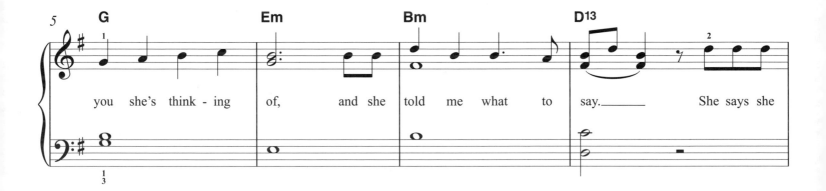

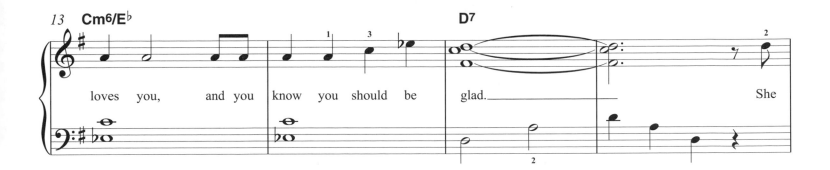

13 Cm6/E♭   D7

loves   you,   and you   know   you   should   be   glad._____   She

17 Em   A7   2

loves   you,   yeah,   yeah,   yeah.   She   loves   you,   yeah,   yeah,   yeah. And with a

³⁄₅

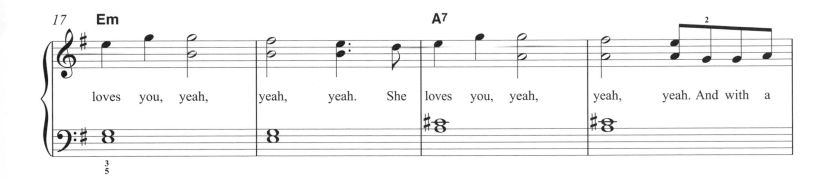

21 Cm6/E♭   Daug7   D7   G   2

love   like   that,   you   know   you   should   be   glad._____   She

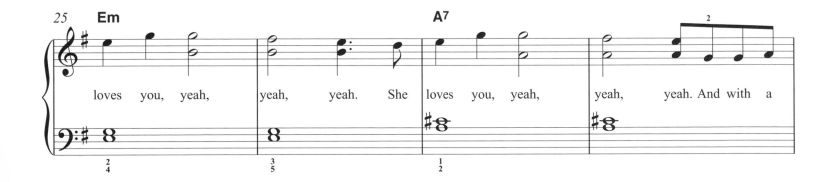

25 Em   A7   2

loves   you,   yeah,   yeah,   yeah.   She   loves   you,   yeah,   yeah,   yeah. And with a

²⁄₄   ³⁄₅   ¹⁄₂

29 Cm6/E♭   Daug7   D7   G

love   like   that,   you   know   you   should   be   glad._____

Something

Words and Music by George Harrison

The idea for this song came to George after listening to a song by James Taylor.
'Something' would become the most enduring track from the *Abbey Road* album.
Indeed, it was recorded by Frank Sinatra, who called it "the greatest love song ever written".

Hints & Tips: Practice bars 9 and 10 first. Watch out for the change of key signature (A major) at bar 11.

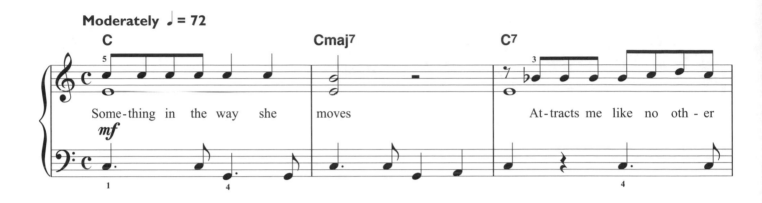

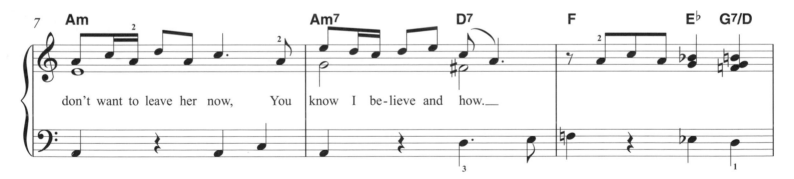

know,__ I don't know.   You stick a-round now, it may show,   I don't

know,__ I don't know.   Some-thing in the way she   knows

And all I have to do is   think of her.   Some-thing in the things she

shows me.   I   don't want to leave her now,   You   know I be-lieve and how.__

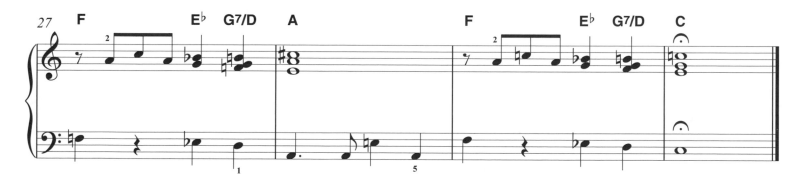

Strawberry Fields Forever

Words and Music by John Lennon and Paul McCartney

Written about one of Lennon's old Liverpool haunts, Strawberry Field referred to a Salvation Army home he would often visit in his upbringing. The band recorded two versions of this song, in different keys and tempos, for Lennon to choose between. Eventually, after agonizing over both, he instead called up producer George Martin, requesting them to be glued together! Amazingly, Martin pulled it off by slowing down and down-tuning the faster version — you can hear the track merge from one to the other 1 minute into the song.

Hints & Tips: You should definitely try each hand on its own first, as there are some awkward accidentals (sharps and flats). There are also some odd rhythms and changes of tempo. Have a listen to the song.

Slowly, but not dragging ♩ = 84

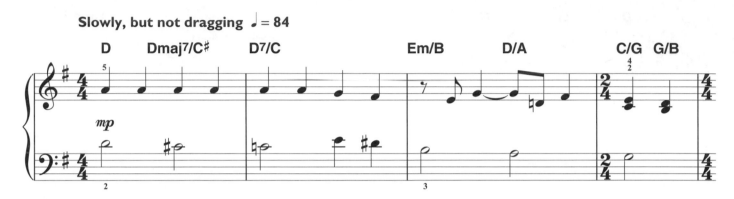

Let me take you down 'cause I'm go - in' to Straw - ber - ry

Fields. Noth - ing is real, and noth - ing to get hung a - bout.

Straw - ber - ry Fields___ for - ev - er.___

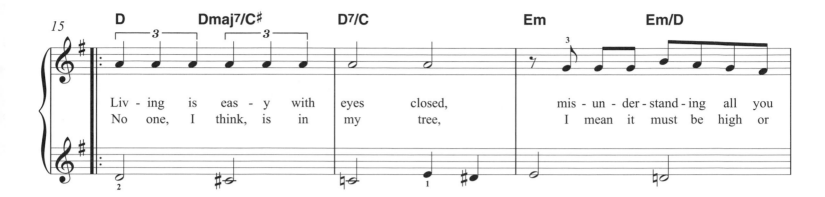

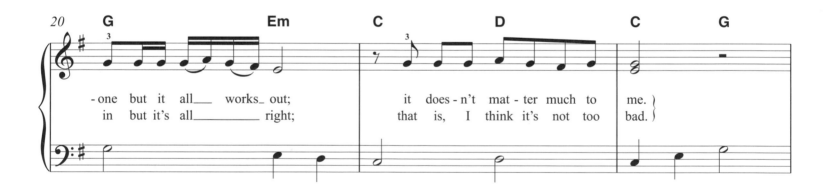

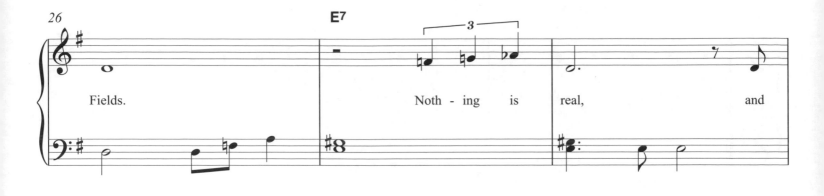

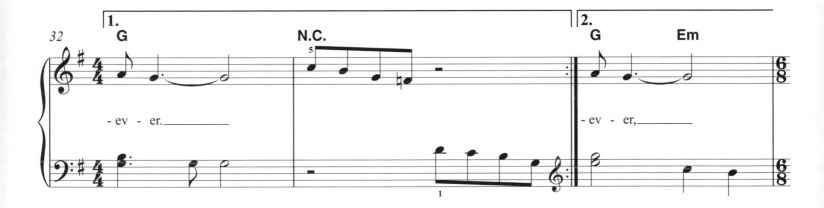

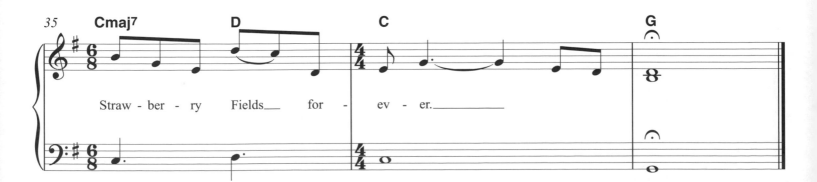

When I'm Sixty-Four

Words and Music by John Lennon and Paul McCartney

This satire on getting old was actually composed by McCartney when he was only 16. The engineers
at Abbey Road made his voice sound more youthful by speeding the voice track up a notch.

Hints & Tips: If you can swing the quavers (eighth notes) in this piece, it will add to the
jazzy character. The piece should be quite jaunty and have an almost comical quality!

We Can Work It Out

Words and Music by John Lennon and Paul McCartney

Released as a double A-side along with 'Day Tripper' in 1965, McCartney wrote this about his then-girlfriend, Jane Asher. His optimistic, upbeat take on the subject was counteracted by Lennon's addition to the song – the section that starts with "life is very short". The couple was together for 5 years in total. This track was one of the longest taken to record for the band, totalling about 11 hours over two days!

Hints & Tips: The meter of this song is quite straightforward at first, but changes dramatically in bars 13—14 and again at bars 19—20. Keep the triplets steady and choose a medium tempo.

Life is ver-y short and there's no time_____ for fuss-ing and

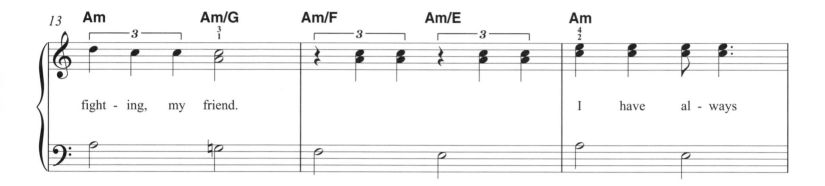

fight - ing, my friend. I have al - ways

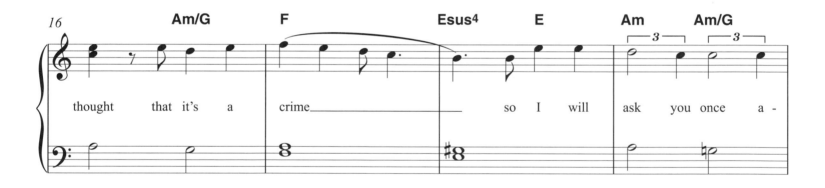

thought that it's a crime_____ so I will ask you once a -

D.C. al Coda

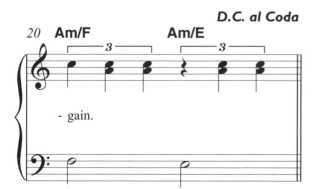

- gain.

⊕ Coda

While My Guitar Gently Weeps

Words and Music by George Harrison

Though he is not credited, fellow musician Eric Clapton is heard playing the lead guitar on this track written by George Harrison. Initially, Harrison found it hard to convince Lennon and McCartney to take the song seriously, until he invited Clapton to the studio to record it, at which point the rest of the band warmed to it. 'While My Guitar Gently Weeps' was included on *The White Album,* 1968, when the band was increasingly showing signs of tension as their career in the spotlight started to take its toll.

Hints & Tips: This song starts in G minor (B♭ and E♭ in the key signature) but moves into the major at bar 17. Practice the left hand on its own at first — two notes together for most of the song.

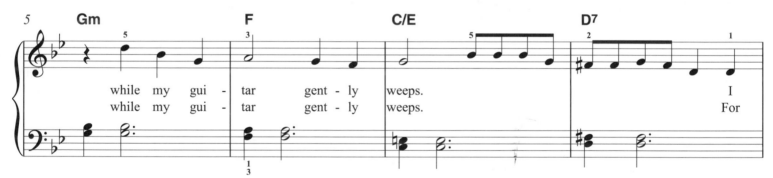

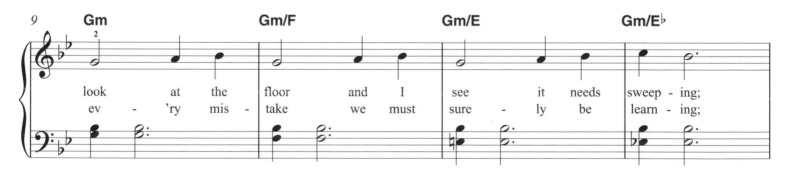

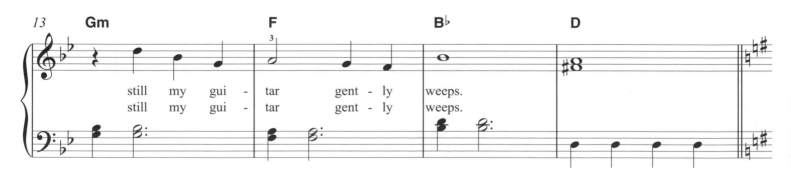

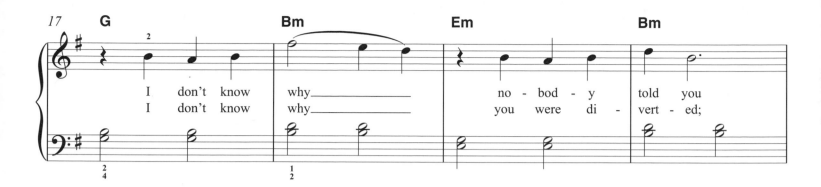

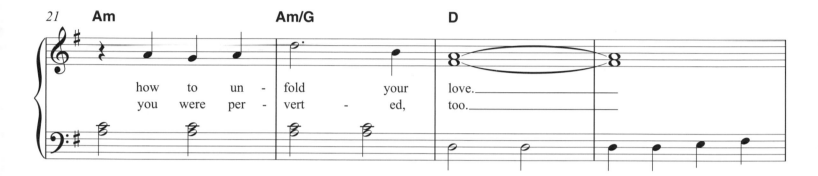

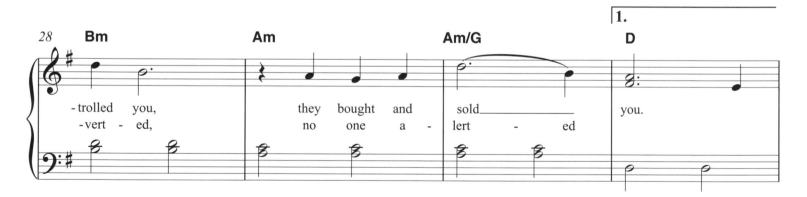

With a Little Help From My Friends

Words and Music by John Lennon and Paul McCartney

'With a Little Help From My Friends' was sung by drummer
Ringo Starr on the *Sgt. Pepper's Lonely Hearts Club Band* album.

Hints & Tips: The melody falls in a very limited range, enabling you to play the first two pages with only slight
adjustments to your right-hand position. Play the melody with swung quavers (eighth notes) as indicated. This tune
is constructed from four-bar phrases that often repeat twice or more. Noticing this will help you learn the song quickly.

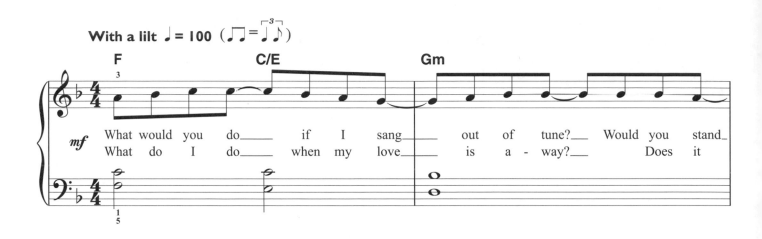

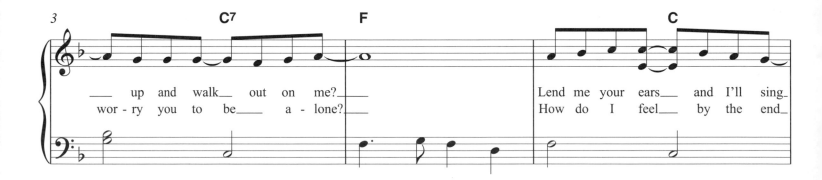

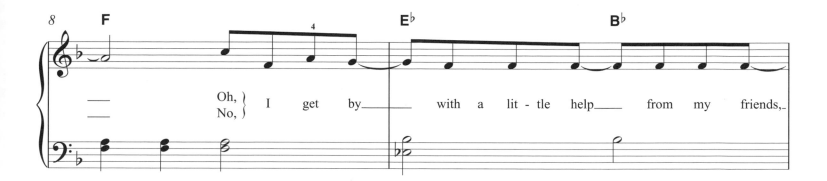

Oh, } I get by___ with a lit-tle help___ from my friends,___
No, }

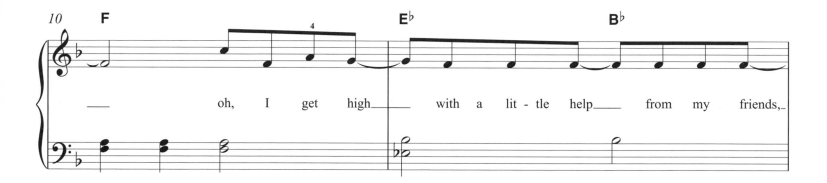

oh, I get high___ with a lit-tle help___ from my friends,___

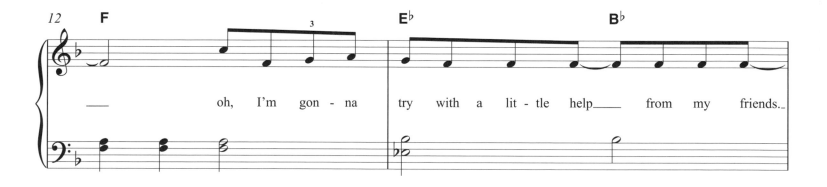

oh, I'm gon - na try with a lit-tle help___ from my friends.___

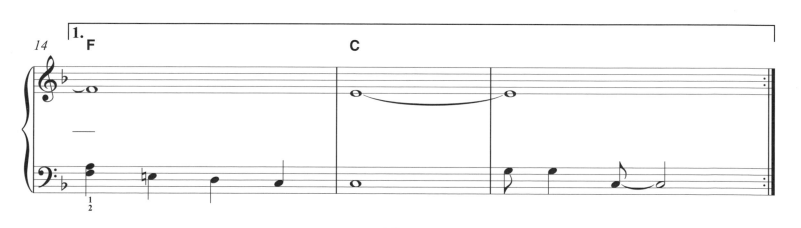

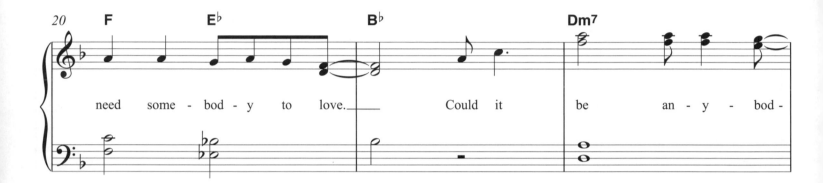

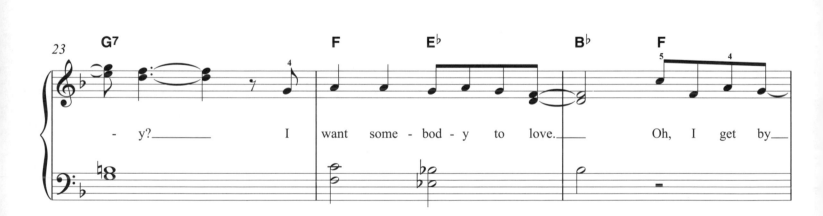

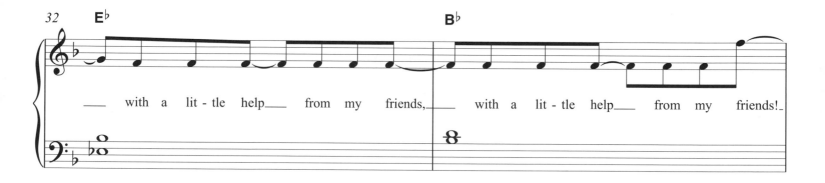

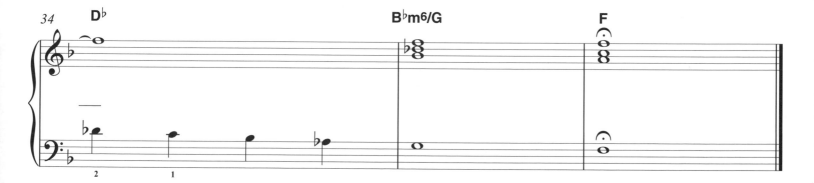

Ticket to Ride

Words and Music by John Lennon and Paul McCartney

Released in April 1965 as a single, 'Ticket to Ride' has the distinction of being the first Beatles song to play longer than three minutes. It also, of course, reached No. 1 in the UK chart and spent three weeks in the top slot.

Hints & Tips: This piece works best if it is played with tremendous energy. Practice bars that have the melody and harmony parts moving together (e.g. bars 2, 4 and 27) with hands separately and very slowly.

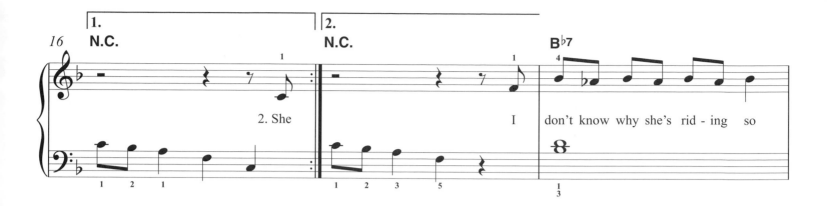

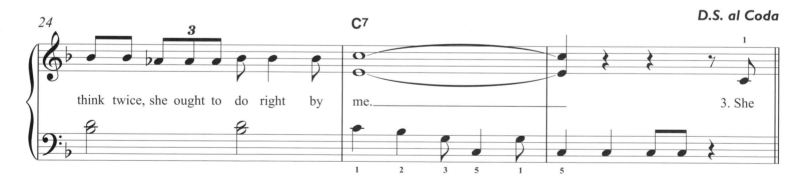

Twist and Shout

Words and Music by Bert Russell and Phil Medley

After running himself ragged with a 12-hour day in the studio, Lennon was barely able to sing by the time the band were looking to record 'Twist and Shout'. However, he summoned up his energy, took a couple of throat lozenges and went for the take! This track was a big hit in live sets – so much so that it is said the band often could not hear themselves play over the relentless screaming fans.

Hints & Tips: This song is in D major, so watch the two sharps in the key signature: F and C. The lyrics in brackets are backing vocals which could be played slightly softer, like an echo.

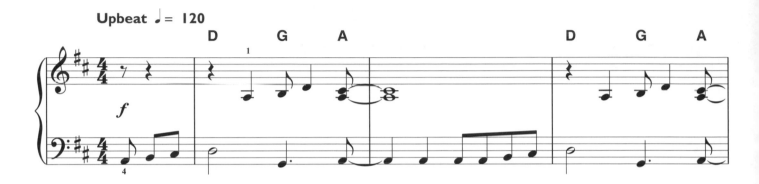

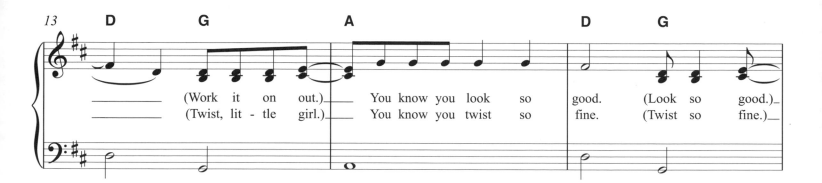

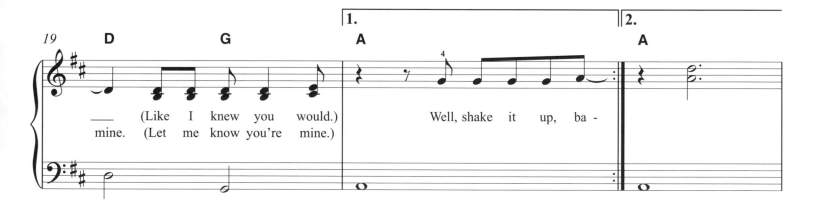

Yellow Submarine

Words and Music by John Lennon and Paul McCartney

Ringo, unusually, sings lead vocal on this track. The melange of different watery
sound effects and even a brass band shows that the group were moving
further and further away from a recording style that could be reproduced live.

Hints & Tips: The chords in the left hand at the beginning can be played with quite a heavy tone.
These chords give the piece a sea shanty-type feel and are very important to obtain the right character.

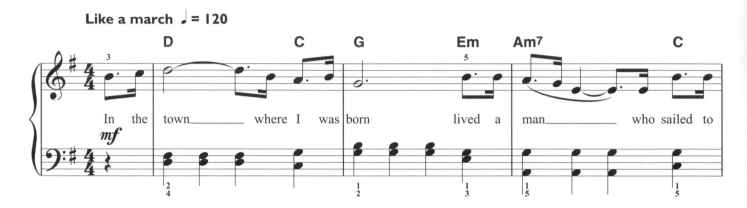

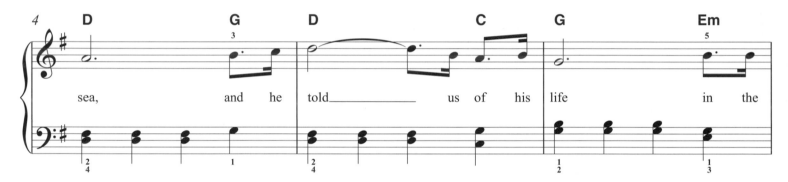

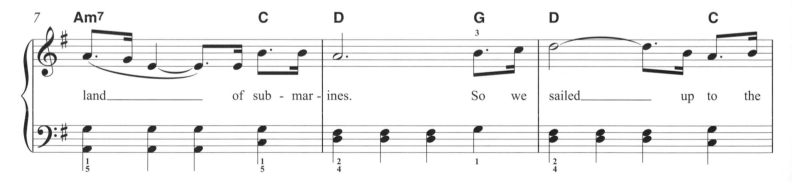

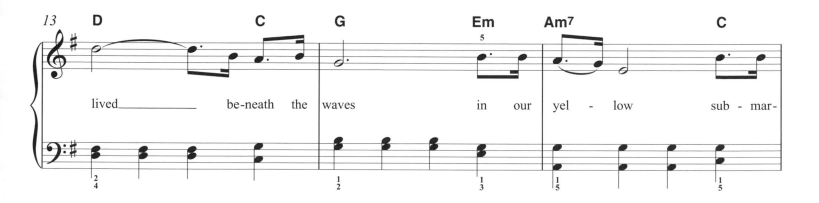

lived_____ be-neath the waves   in our yel - low   sub - mar-

-ine.   We all live in a   yel - low sub - mar-ine,

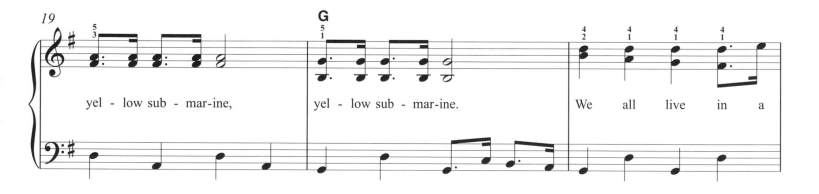

yel - low sub - mar-ine,   yel - low sub - mar-ine.   We all live   in a

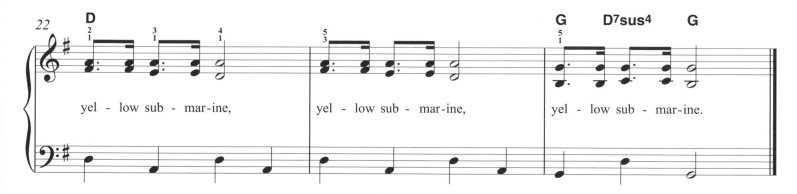

yel - low sub - mar-ine,   yel - low sub - mar - ine,   yel - low sub - mar-ine.

Yesterday

Words and Music by John Lennon and Paul McCartney

One of The Beatles' most popular ballads, this song started life with the title 'Scrambled Eggs' after Paul woke from a dream with the tune in his head but with the alternative couplet "Scrambled eggs, oh, darling, I love your legs".

Hints & Tips: This song is full of scalic passages. Practice them slowly at first, paying attention to all the accidentals, then try to give each of them a natural flow. They could rise and fall in dynamic as the pitches rise and fall, it's up to you!

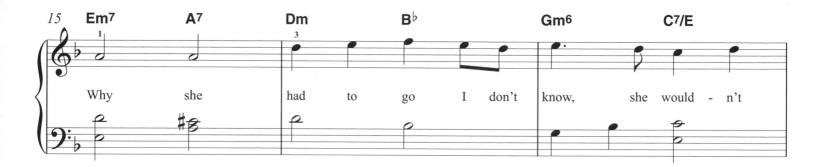

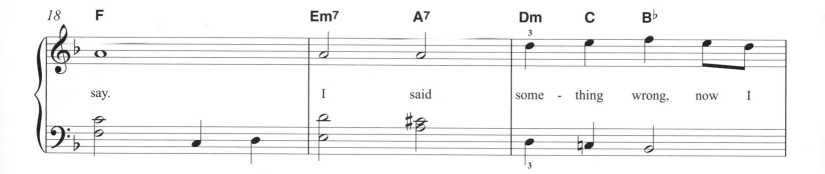

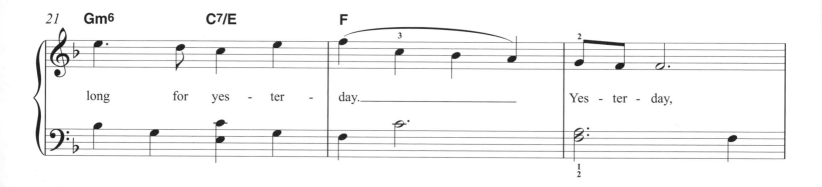

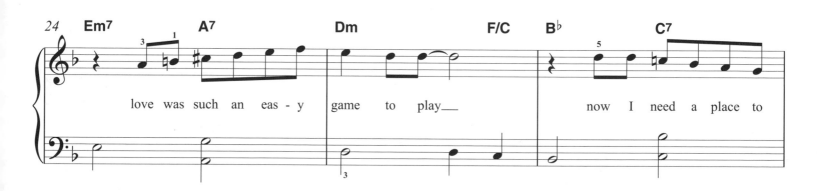

Discover our range of really easy piano bumper books...

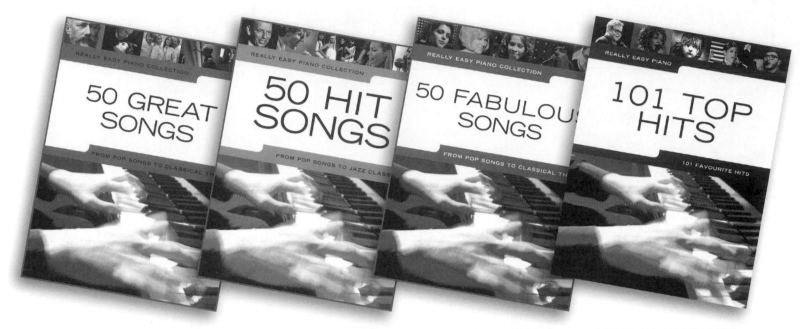

ORDER NO. AM995643   ORDER NO. AM1000615   ORDER NO. AM999449   ORDER NO. AM1008975

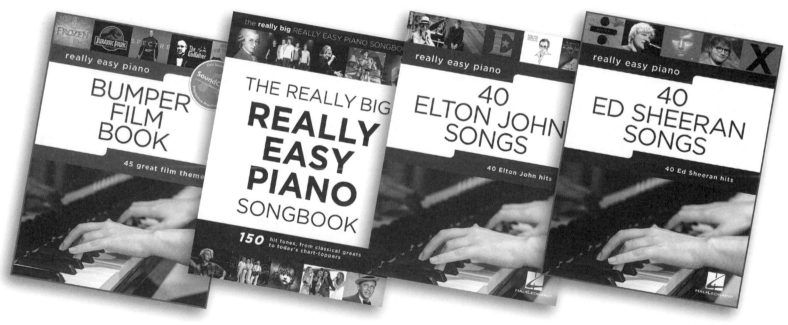

ORDER NO. HLE90004915   ORDER NO. AM1011032   ORDER NO. HL00295382   ORDER NO. HL00287156

Just visit your local music shop and ask
to see our huge range of music in print.